First World War
and Army of Occupation
War Diary
France, Belgium and Germany

38 DIVISION
Divisional Troops
121 Brigade Royal Field Artillery
1 January 1916 - 1 April 1919

WO95/2546/3

The Naval & Military Press Ltd
www.nmarchive.com
Published in association with The National Archives

Published by

The Naval & Military Press Ltd

Unit 10 Ridgewood Industrial Park,

Uckfield, East Sussex,

TN22 5QE England

Tel: +44 (0) 1825 749494

www.naval-military-press.com

www.nmarchive.com

This diary has been reprinted in facsimile from the original. Any imperfections are inevitably reproduced and the quality may fall short of modern type and cartographic standards.

© **Crown Copyright**
Images reproduced by permission of The National Archives, London, England, 2015.

Contents

Document type	Place/Title	Date From	Date To
Heading	WO95/2546/3		
Heading	38th Division Divl Artillery 121st Brigade R.F.A. 1915 Dec-Apr 1919		
War Diary	121st Bde. R.F.A. Vol I 23.D.15 31st Jan 16		
Miscellaneous	121st Brigade R.F.A. March Orders.	23/12/1915	23/12/1915
War Diary		07/02/1916	27/02/1916
Miscellaneous	Appendix 1		
Miscellaneous	Appendix II		
Miscellaneous	Appendix III	23/02/1916	23/02/1916
Miscellaneous	Appendix IV	24/02/1916	24/02/1916
Miscellaneous	Appendix V	24/02/1916	24/02/1916
Miscellaneous	Appendix VI	24/02/1916	24/02/1916
Miscellaneous	Appendix VII	26/02/1916	26/02/1916
Heading	121 R.F.A. Vol 3		
War Diary	Givenchy Sector	01/03/1916	29/03/1916
War Diary		08/03/1916	17/03/1916
War Diary		01/03/1916	14/03/1916
War Diary		11/03/1916	28/04/1916
War Diary		26/04/1916	26/04/1916
War Diary		20/03/1916	23/04/1916
War Diary		04/04/1916	31/05/1916
War Diary	In The Field.	01/06/1916	27/06/1916
Heading	38th Div. XV. Corps. Division Transferred from II. Corps, Fourth Army, 3.7.16. War Diary Headquarters, 121st Brigade. R.F.A. July 1916 Attached : Appendices 1, 2, 3, 4 & 5		
War Diary		01/07/1916	31/07/1916
Miscellaneous	Appendix (1) Operation Order.	06/07/1916	06/07/1916
Miscellaneous	(Para 2 (a)) which will be maintained till 8.30 a.m	07/07/1916	07/07/1916
Miscellaneous	Operation Order. Area for tonight firing July 9/10th Appendix (3)	09/07/1916	09/07/1916
Miscellaneous	Operation Order Appendix (4)	10/07/1916	10/07/1916
Miscellaneous	Appendix (2) Operation Order		
Miscellaneous	MB.574. Reference 1/20,000 Montauban & XV Corps Special 2nd Line Map, attached Appendix (5)	11/07/1916	11/07/1916
Miscellaneous	Table "B" Barrages.		
Miscellaneous	Table "A"		
Miscellaneous	Barrage "E"		
Map			
War Diary	Sailly-Au-Bois	03/08/1916	07/08/1916
War Diary	Authie	08/08/1916	08/08/1916
War Diary	Hem-(Doullens)	11/08/1916	11/08/1916
War Diary	Zeggers Cappel	14/08/1916	14/08/1916
War Diary		06/08/1916	29/08/1916
War Diary	Ypres	20/08/1916	29/08/1916
Miscellaneous	Artillery Programme-August 7th, 1916	07/08/1916	07/08/1916
Operation(al) Order(s)	Operation Order No. 2. Programme For 3rd August, 1916	03/08/1916	03/08/1916
War Diary	Elverdinghe	21/08/1916	28/08/1916
War Diary		21/08/1916	31/08/1916

Type	Description	Start	End
Miscellaneous	38th Divisional Artillery Draft Operation Orders	08/09/1916	08/09/1916
Miscellaneous	X Day		
Miscellaneous	Z Day		
Miscellaneous	Programme For "Z" Night		
Miscellaneous	R.A. 38th Divl No. G.S. 866	15/09/1916	15/09/1916
Miscellaneous	OS.C. Batteries. Left Group R.F.A.	15/09/1916	15/09/1916
War Diary	Proven	01/09/1916	22/09/1916
War Diary	Brielen	22/09/1916	30/09/1916
War Diary	Brielen	28/09/1916	28/09/1916
Miscellaneous	A Raid will take place on the Enemy's trenches on the night of through the gap existing at C.14.a.3.2		
War Diary	Fired	01/09/1916	30/09/1916
Miscellaneous	B/121 War Diary.	00/09/1916	00/09/1916
Miscellaneous	Left Group R.F.A. 38th D.A.	09/09/1916	09/09/1916
Miscellaneous	R.A. 38th Division No. G.S.861	14/09/1916	14/09/1916
Operation(al) Order(s)	Operation Order No. 1. By Lieut., Col., P.J. Paterson D.S.O., R.F.A., Commanding 119th Brigade R.F.A., 38th Divisional Arty.	18/09/1916	18/09/1916
Miscellaneous	OS.C.Batteries, Left Group R.F.A.	19/09/1916	19/09/1916
War Diary		01/09/1916	30/09/1916
War Diary	La Brique Left Sec. In Action At I.2.a.8.5. O.P. Frascati (C.26.a.7.6) Wagon Line Near Hamhoek	01/10/1916	04/10/1916
War Diary	Ypres	05/10/1916	16/10/1916
War Diary	La Brique	17/10/1916	22/10/1916
War Diary	Brielen	10/10/1916	31/10/1916
Miscellaneous		10/10/1916	10/10/1916
Miscellaneous	Minnie	09/10/1916	09/10/1916
Miscellaneous	O.C. D/119th Brigade R.F.A.	12/10/1916	12/10/1916
Miscellaneous	Reference St. Julien Trench Map. Scale 1/10,000. Edition 3D.		
Miscellaneous			
Miscellaneous	O.C. Brigade R.F.A.	13/10/1916	13/10/1916
Miscellaneous	Brigade Major, R.A., 38th Division.	12/10/1916	12/10/1916
Miscellaneous	Raid "B" Amendments.		
Miscellaneous	A Raid will take place at C.13.b.9.7 on the night of the 13th-14th Oct.	13/10/1916	13/10/1916
Miscellaneous	O.C. Brigade R.F.A.	14/10/1916	14/10/1916
Operation(al) Order(s)	Operation Order No 6 A.	28/10/1916	28/10/1916
Operation(al) Order(s)	Operation Order No. 8	28/10/1916	28/10/1916
Operation(al) Order(s)	Operation Order-No. 7	26/10/1916	26/10/1916
Miscellaneous		31/10/1916	31/10/1916
War Diary		09/10/1916	13/10/1916
War Diary	Brielen	01/11/1916	30/11/1916
War Diary		10/11/1916	29/11/1916
Miscellaneous	Caesar	11/11/1916	11/11/1916
Miscellaneous	O.C. A/121st Brigade R.F.A.	10/11/1916	10/11/1916
Operation(al) Order(s)	Operation Order No. 10	14/11/1916	14/11/1916
Miscellaneous	A Raid will be carried out on High Command Redoubt by the 14th (Welsh) Regt. on X day.		
War Diary	Poperinghe	01/12/1916	16/12/1916
War Diary	Watou	25/12/1916	31/12/1916
War Diary	Elverdinghe	01/12/1916	15/12/1916
War Diary		01/01/1916	31/01/1916
War Diary		21/01/1916	21/01/1916
War Diary		17/01/1916	31/01/1916
War Diary	Ypres (28.I.2.C.9.2) 3 Guns In Action No 1, 2 & 4	01/12/1916	11/12/1916

Type	Description	Start	End
War Diary	Ypres	12/12/1916	15/12/1916
Heading	War Diary D/121. (1/12/16-15/12/16.) Adjutant 121st Bde RFA		
War Diary		01/01/1917	30/01/1917
War Diary	Wissant	01/01/1917	31/01/1917
War Diary	Trois Tours	03/02/1917	03/02/1917
War Diary	Trois Tours	01/02/1917	27/02/1917
War Diary	Trois Tours	19/02/1917	19/02/1917
War Diary		17/02/1917	27/02/1917
Operation(al) Order(s)	Operation Order No. 15	03/02/1917	03/02/1917
Operation(al) Order(s)	Operation Order No. 21		
Operation(al) Order(s)	Amendments & Additions to Operation Order No. 21		
Operation(al) Order(s)	Addition To Operation Order No. 21	16/02/1917	16/02/1917
Operation(al) Order(s)	Amendments (2) to Operation Order No. 21	16/02/1917	16/02/1917
War Diary	Trois Tours	01/03/1917	31/03/1917
War Diary		13/03/1917	31/03/1917
War Diary		01/03/1917	22/03/1917
War Diary		04/03/1917	28/03/1917
War Diary	In The Field	21/03/1917	01/05/1917
War Diary	Brielen	01/04/1917	01/05/1917
War Diary		05/04/1917	13/04/1917
War Diary		04/04/1917	30/04/1917
War Diary		01/04/1917	30/04/1917
War Diary	Trois. Tours Chateau.	01/05/1917	01/05/1917
War Diary	Brielen	04/05/1917	15/05/1917
War Diary	Elverdinghe	21/05/1917	31/05/1917
Operation(al) Order(s)	Operation Order No. 1 Right Group-38th Divisional Artillery.	07/05/1917	07/05/1917
Operation(al) Order(s)	Appendix to Operation Order No. 1. Right Group-38th Divisional Artillery.	14/05/1917	14/05/1917
Operation(al) Order(s)	Operation Order No. 1. Left Group-38th D.A.	24/05/1917	24/05/1917
Operation(al) Order(s)	Left Group-38th D.A. Operation Order No. 3	27/05/1917	27/05/1917
Operation(al) Order(s)	Left Group-38th D.A. Operation Order No. 5	29/05/1917	29/05/1917
Miscellaneous	H.G. 28	29/05/1917	29/05/1917
War Diary	Field	01/05/1917	31/05/1917
Operation(al) Order(s)	L 11 Copy A.D.A Operation Order No. 3	07/11/1917	07/11/1917
War Diary	Elverdinghe Chateau	03/06/1917	09/06/1917
War Diary	Elverdinghe	08/06/1917	19/06/1917
War Diary	Hamhoek	19/06/1917	19/06/1917
Miscellaneous	Amendment to Artillery Raid Programme.		
Miscellaneous	Left Group-38th D.A. Artillery Programme		
Miscellaneous	Left Group-38th D.A.	01/12/1917	01/12/1917
Miscellaneous	Left Group 38th D.A.	05/12/1917	05/12/1917
Operation(al) Order(s)	Right Group 38th. D.A. Operation Order No. 33	07/06/1917	07/06/1917
Operation(al) Order(s)	38th Divisional Artillery Operation Order No. 68	06/06/1917	06/06/1917
Operation(al) Order(s)	38th Divisional Artillery Operation Order No. 67		
Operation(al) Order(s)	Left Group 38th D.A. Operation Order No. 6	06/06/1917	06/06/1917
Miscellaneous	EG.54	04/06/1917	04/06/1917
Miscellaneous	Harassing Fire	03/06/1917	03/06/1917
Operation(al) Order(s)	Addition To 38th Divisional Artillery O.O. No. 68	01/06/1917	01/06/1917
Miscellaneous	Appendix 2. Programme for "A"/121, "B"/121, Enfilade Section "B"/122, "D"/121 and "D"/122		
Miscellaneous	Rates Of Fire.	02/06/1917	02/06/1917
Miscellaneous	EG.37	01/06/1917	01/06/1917
Miscellaneous	R.A. VIII Corps No. RA/746/55. R.A. 38th Division No. G.S.2190	02/05/1917	02/05/1917

Type	Description	Start	End
Operation(al) Order(s)	38th. Divisional Artillery Operation Order No. 65	08/06/1917	08/06/1917
Miscellaneous	EG.68	08/06/1917	08/06/1917
Miscellaneous	EG.61		
Operation(al) Order(s)	O.O.33		
War Diary	Elverdinghe	29/08/1916	31/08/1916
War Diary	Armentieres	00/10/1917	00/10/1917
Operation(al) Order(s)	Left Group-38th D.A. Operation Order No. 1	06/10/1917	06/10/1917
Miscellaneous		13/10/1917	13/10/1917
Miscellaneous	Left Group 38 Div. AD 307		
Miscellaneous	Left Group. 38 Div AD 306		
War Diary	Left Group 38 DA AD 308	20/10/1917	20/10/1917
Operation(al) Order(s)	Left Group 38 DA. Operation Order No. 2	28/10/1917	28/10/1917
Miscellaneous	Proposed Artillery Action During Gas Projection.		
Operation(al) Order(s)	38th (Welsh) Division Order No 146	27/10/1917	27/10/1917
Miscellaneous	Brigade Order.	27/10/1917	27/10/1917
War Diary	Armentieres	07/11/1917	24/11/1917
Operation(al) Order(s)	Left Group-38th D.A. Operation Order No. 3	06/11/1917	06/11/1917
Operation(al) Order(s)	Extract from Counter Battery Office XI Corps Operation Order No. 34	07/11/1917	07/11/1917
Operation(al) Order(s)	Counter Battery Office, XIth Corps. Operation Order No. 34	07/11/1917	07/11/1917
Miscellaneous	Left Group		
Miscellaneous	AD.045	07/11/1917	07/11/1917
Miscellaneous	Left Group 38th D.A. Instructions No 7	27/11/1917	27/11/1917
Miscellaneous	Left Group. D.T.M.O.	24/11/1917	24/11/1917
War Diary	Armentieres	01/12/1917	01/01/1918
War Diary	In The Field	01/01/1918	28/01/1918
War Diary	Haverskerque	01/02/1918	15/02/1918
War Diary	Near Armentieres	15/02/1918	01/03/1918
War Diary	Armentieres	01/03/1918	29/03/1918
Heading	38th Div. V. Corps. War Diary Headquarters. 121st Brigade R.F.A. April 1918		
War Diary	Erquinghem	01/04/1918	09/04/1918
War Diary	Steenwercke	10/04/1918	10/04/1918
War Diary	La Creche	11/04/1918	11/04/1918
War Diary	Bailleul	11/04/1918	13/04/1918
War Diary	S. Jans. Cappel	14/04/1918	15/04/1918
War Diary	Berthen.	16/04/1918	24/04/1918
War Diary	Abeele Hamhoek	25/04/1918	25/04/1918
War Diary	Reninghelst	25/04/1918	07/05/1918
War Diary	Dickebusch	08/05/1918	12/05/1918
War Diary	Haandekot	18/05/1918	18/05/1918
War Diary	Gezaincourt	00/05/1918	00/05/1918
War Diary	Raincheval	01/06/1918	11/06/1918
War Diary	Englebelmer	13/06/1918	23/06/1918
Miscellaneous	Left Group. Right Group. D.T.M.C. S.C.R.A.,	15/06/1918	15/06/1918
War Diary	Englebelmer	11/07/1918	27/07/1918
War Diary	Harponville	01/08/1918	31/08/1918
War Diary	Morval	01/09/1918	01/09/1918
War Diary	Mouchoir Copse	02/09/1918	03/09/1918
War Diary	Sailly Saillissel	04/09/1918	04/09/1918
War Diary	Rocquigny	05/09/1918	05/09/1918
War Diary	Lechelle	06/09/1918	06/09/1918
War Diary	Ytres	07/09/1918	07/09/1918
War Diary	Fins	08/09/1918	30/09/1918
War Diary	Villers-Guislain	01/10/1918	04/10/1918

War Diary	La Terriere	05/10/1918	07/10/1918
War Diary	Mortho Wood	08/10/1918	08/10/1918
War Diary	Hurtevent Farms W of Bertry	09/10/1918	09/10/1918
War Diary	E of Troisville	10/10/1918	12/10/1918
War Diary	Troisville	15/10/1918	19/10/1918
War Diary	Montay	21/10/1918	22/10/1918
War Diary	Ovillers	23/10/1918	23/10/1918
War Diary	Paul Jacques Farm	24/10/1918	26/10/1918
War Diary	Bertry	27/10/1918	31/10/1918
War Diary	Poix Du Nord.	01/11/1918	04/11/1918
War Diary	Hecq	04/11/1918	05/11/1918
War Diary	Sarbaras	06/11/1918	20/11/1918
War Diary	Aulnoye	01/12/1918	01/01/1919
War Diary	Pont Noyelles	01/01/1919	20/03/1919
War Diary	Glisy	31/03/1919	01/04/1919

WC95/3546/3.

38TH DIVISION
DIVL ARTILLERY

121ST BRIGADE R.F.A.

~~JAN 1916~~ - APR 1919.
1915 DEC

121st Bde. R.F.A.
Vol I

2 3. R. 15 —
31st Jan. 16

Jan .16
Apr .16

WAR DIARY of 131st Brigade R.F.A.

Army Form C. 2118

INTELLIGENCE SUMMARY

(Erase heading not required.)

Instructions regarding War Diaries and Intelligence Summaries are contained in F.S. Regs., Part II. and the Staff Manual respectively. Title Pages will be prepared in manuscript.

Place	Date	Hour	Summary of Events and Information	Remarks and references to Appendices
			March Orders. 23-12-15	
			The Brigade will march to No. 2 Gate, Southampton Docks to-morrow.	
			Route: Via Winchester, Eastleigh, Chandlersford.	
			Hours of starting and Berth at which embarking as under.	
			Starting point South end of Avenue.	

Unit.	Hour of starting	Arr: at No.2 Dock Gate.	Berth
H.Q. & A. Battery	5.15. A.M.	10-30. A.M.	32.
B.A.C.	5.25. A.M.	10-50. A.M.	46.
B. Battery	6.45. A.M.	12- noon	32
C. Battery	8.15 A.M.	1-30. P.M.	32
D. Battery	9.35 A.M.	2-50 P.M.	32

WAR DIARY of 121st Brigade. R.F.A.

INTELLIGENCE SUMMARY (2) (cont.)

(Erase heading not required.)

Place	Date	Hour	Summary of Events and Information	Remarks and references to Appendices

The Headquarters and Batteries arrived punctually at the Dock Gates and proceeded to embark.

At 5 P.M. 23-12-15. The boat left Southampton Docks for Havre.

Arriving at Havre Harbour the next morning 24-12-15. The Brigade disembarked and waited in the Docks yard until it moved off by Batteries to the Station for entraining.

Arriving at Moeuvres on 25-12-15. Batteries moved to Bettes.

On the 31-12-15. 2 Officers and 30 men per Battery were attached to units of the 19th Div. R.F.A. and proceeded to firing line for instruction. The Brigade relieved the By. th Bde (who were in action)

WAR DIARY of 121st Brigade R.F.A.
INTELLIGENCE SUMMARY (3) (cont)

On the 30/31st January 1916, and were attached to the Left Group 38th Div. Commanded by Lt. Col. N.F. Laing to R.F.A.

[signature]
Bgr 121st Bde RFA

7/2/16

WAR DIARY
or
INTELLIGENCE SUMMARY

(Erase heading not required.)

Army Form C. 2118

121 Bde R.F.A. February 1916

Place	Date	Hour	Summary of Events and Information	Remarks and references to Appendices
	7th & 8th Feb		On the nights of Feb 7th and 8th a scheme was arranged to destroy the enemys working party in the orchard S.W. of BOIS DU BIEZ this was successfully carried out, not ceasing for several days.	
	8th		Another Bombardment was successfully carried out in the afternoon of the 8th. considerable damage was done to the enemys parapet. Part of which was set on fire, a gap being made of 10 yards.	
	16th Feb		On the 16th Feb the Left Group, 38th Bde Artillery, relieved 13 Group 2nd D. Division who were in action in Givenchy area, and became Right Group, 38th Divl Arty, under the command of Lieut Colonel H.G Pringle R.F.A.	
	16th		B Battery were then split up so the position taken over by this group were six gun Batteries. Half of 'C' going to B/121st and half to D/121st making these Batteries six gun Batteries instead of four.	

Army Form C. 2118

WAR DIARY
INTELLIGENCE SUMMARY
(Erase heading not required.)

Instructions regarding War Diaries and Intelligence Summaries are contained in F.S. Regs., Part II. and the Staff Manual respectively. Title Pages will be prepared in manuscript.

Place	Date	Hour	Summary of Events and Information	Remarks and references to Appendices
	18th		The troops then consisted of A/121st four gun Battery, B/121st six gun Battery, D/121st six gun Battery, A/120th four gun Battery B/122nd and half of A/122nd making a six gun (Howitzer) Battery and four six inch Howitzers.	
	19th		On the 19th Feb (see appendices 1 & 2) a bombardment took place to cover registration by the French Hows.	
	23rd		On the 23rd (Appendix III) in conjunction with the French Mortar Battery no.67. A scheme was arranged and fire was carried on trench junctions.	
	24th		On the 24th (Appendix IV, V, VI) An Offensive Programme for the purpose of wire cutting was carried out by N. Battery R.H.A. B/121st and A/122nd. A lane of 15 feet was cut at A.9.c.6/2.6. Information was received on the 24th by a German Deserter that reliefs were taking place on the nights of the 25th. A scheme was arranged and carried out at 7.30 pm. Battery Salvos being fired at regular intervals, averaging 10 minutes on all Roads, Trench Junctions &c.	

1895. Wt. W593/826 1,000,000 4/15 J.B.C. & A. A.D.S.S./Forms/C. 2118.

WAR DIARY or INTELLIGENCE SUMMARY

Army Form C. 2118

Place	Date	Hour	Summary of Events and Information	Remarks and references to Appendices
	26th		On the 26th (Appendix VII) a bombardment of the German Salient at A.9.b. by the 28th Siege Battery and flight group, 35th R.H. Arty., considerable damage was done to the enemy's parapet in several places.	
	27th		On the night of the 27th a programme was carried out by the Right Group, 38th R.H. Arty. N. Battery R.H.A. in conjunction with B/122 and B/121st endeavoured to increase the Southern gap which had previously been made at A.9.c.1 1/2. 1/2.	

M Burnhy Myn
Lg 121st Bde Bry

3/2/16

WAR DIARY
INTELLIGENCE SUMMARY
(Erase heading not required.)

Army Form C. 2118

Place	Date	Hour	Summary of Events and Information	Remarks and references to Appendices

Appendix I 7.30pm 18th & 19th Feb

The Germans are due to carry out reliefs tonight. The following programme will be carried out starting at 7.30 p.m. Battery also being fired at irregular intervals averaging 10 mins.

A/121st IX. A.10.a.6.0. – A.10.d.1/2.9.
         IX. A.11.R.4.6. – A.11.b.2.–5 1/2.

B/121st IX. A.10.c.3.3 1/2. – A.10.C.9.3.
         IX on Corps Roads A.11.c.8 1/2.3 1/2. HE
         IX on A.11.b.8 1/2.3 1/2 – A.11.b.8.2

P/121st IX A.10.b.2.8 – A.10.b.8 1/2.8 1/2
         IX. A.4.c.9 1/2.2. – A.4.d.3.1 1/2
         IX on house A.4.c.5 1/2.3. HE

P/120th IX. A.10.b.2.6. – A.11.a.1/2.1.
         IX tram lines A.4.c.6 1/2.2 – A.4.a.1.0.

WAR DIARY
INTELLIGENCE SUMMARY
(Erase heading not required.)

Appendix I contd

N/122nd IX on Cross Roads CANTELEUX.
 IX " " A.10.a 3.5.
 IX Trench junction A.3.d.8.5½.

at 10pm A+B 121st will fire on their right lines at B.F.
10 secs. for 2 mins.

N/120 will barrage German support trench from A.9 to 4½ 4½.
— A.9.d.9.9.

N/122 will fire at the following trench junctions
A.16.a 6.8½. A.10.c.5.½ A.10.B 7.3.
A.10.c.4.8. A.10.a.11½.1. A.10.a. 0.7.

WAR DIARY
INTELLIGENCE SUMMARY
(Erase heading not required.)

Appendix II.

In order to cover registration by trench howr B/121 & B/120 will barrage trenches as under between 10am & 10.15 tomorrow 19-2-16

B/121   1X AUSTRIAN WAY
        1X PRUSSIAN WAY
        1X Support trenches from junction of PRUSSIAN WAY — SAXON WAY.

B/120& German support trenches from A 9 b 4½. 4½.
        to junction with PRUSSIAN WAY.

Rate of fire S.F. 45 secs.

WAR DIARY
INTELLIGENCE SUMMARY
(Erase heading not required.)

APPENDIX III   23-2-16

The heavy trench mortars will fire 10 rounds at trench junction A.9.b.4½.0.
Simultaneously and at intervals to be arranged by the O.C. B/122nd and O.C. by the T.H. Battery. 1 section of B/122nd will fire for 20 seconds at the french junction A.9.b.9.2
1 section will fire 20 rounds at A.9.b.5.3½ — A.9.a.8.4½.4½
B/120 will barrage support trench A.9.b.4½.4½ — A.9.b.b½.½.
and then attacked gun with B/121 will barrage the N edge of the salient from A.9.b.2½.4. — A.9.b.5.5
A/121st 1 section will barrage AUSTRIAN WAY.

APPENDIX IV   24.2.16.

1X. M/20th craters from Hq.6.14b.0. - A.9.a.8½.5.
1X Support trench A.9.b.6.1 - A.10.c.1½.7
A/12 at 1X Barrage PRUSSIAN WAY.
   1X   "   SAXON WAY
13/12½ 1X CT A.10.c.1.3 - A.10.c.3.3½.
       1X CT A.10.c.1.3½ - A.10.c.3.4.

WAR DIARY

INTELLIGENCE SUMMARY

APPENDIX V

24.2-16.

N. Battery R.H.A. will cut wire at A.9.b.6/2.b.
commencing at 2.0 pm 100 rounds will be fired.

D/122nd at 3 pm will fire 30 rounds H.E. and wrench parapet immediately in rear of gap made in the wire.

A/121st at 3.30 pm will fire 30 rounds H.E. at breach made in Parapet by D/122nd.

Fire must cease at 3.45 pm. Parapet will be cleared between streets 60 + 63.

WAR DIARY
or
INTELLIGENCE SUMMARY

Army Form C. 2118

APPENDIX VI   24-2-16.

N. Bty. R.H.A will cut wire about A.10.d.10½.6 commencing at 10am on the 24th inst. It is hoped to cut a gap 15 yards wide with 100 rounds. Immediately after, the 4.5" How: will fire 30 rounds H.E. at German parapet immediately opposite gap in wire and this will be followed by 20 to 30 rounds 18 pr H.E. The operation will last about 1½ hours. The Infantry should co-operate by keeping the gap under machine gun and rifle fire. This gap in wire and parapet will be enlarged at a later date when a similar gap will be made South of Duck's Bill (A.10.0.1½.½).

WAR DIARY or INTELLIGENCE SUMMARY

APPENDIX VII   26 - 27 - 2 - 16.

The following scheme will be carried out by Right Group, 38th Arty Bty Bngde (26th 27th).

A/121
7.30 pm — 1 x salvo at irregular intervals averaging
  20 mins at trench A.9.6.6½.3 – A.9.6.9.4.
10.30 pm — 1 x area A.9.6.7½.6 – A.9.6.6½.6½ – A.9.6.9½.8 – A.9.6.10.7.

B/121 — 1 Gun section at tramway A.9.6.9.1½ – A.10.a.5.8
at 6.25 pm; 6.50 pm; 7 pm; 7.25 pm; 7 pm; 7.40 pm; 8.10 pm; 8.30 pm.

R/121 – This Battery will have an Officer in the O.P. between 6.30 pm – 10.30 pm to watch for any hostile machine guns which may open fire. If located during fire of remaining section to bear. If not sweep German front line between A.9.B.4½.7 and A.3.a.4.5. Salvos of 4 guns at tramway line A.4.c.6.2 – A.4.c.10.½ at 6.30 pm; 6.45 pm; 7.5 pm; 7.8 pm; 7.30 pm; 7.45 pm; 8.10 pm; 9.0 pm.

WAR DIARY
INTELLIGENCE SUMMARY
(Erase heading not required.)

Army Form C. 2118

Place	Date	Hour	Summary of Events and Information	Remarks and references to Appendices
			APPENDIX VII contd.	
	Night		Barrage A.9.b.5.5. – A.9.b.7.2½. at section fire 1 min: from 7.15pm – 8.0pm. at 8.0pm shift barrage to A.9.b 4½.4½ – A.9.b 6½.1 at section fire 30 secs. at 8.30pm shift barrage back to A.9.b.5.5. – A.9.b.7.2½. at section fire 30 secs. at 9.0pm X.t.1 min till 9.30 pm. It called on by the Infantry at any hour go to Battery fire 5 secs. on A.9.b.4½.4½. – A.9.b.6½.1. for 2 mins, then 2 rounds By fire 20 secs. The signal for this will be the word Barrage. If this fire is required and telephone wires cut "N's" will be sent by lamps to WINDY CORNER from both Corners and the word "Barrage" will be sent on the telephone from there.	

WAR DIARY 3

INTELLIGENCE SUMMARY

APPENDIX VII contd.

A/122nd Battery Salvoes at following points:-
1 X cross roads C.14.d. ST ROCH.
1 X Tramway End A.9.d.9.1½.
1 X Junce at A.9.d.1/2.9. at

6.40 pm, 7.10 pm, 7.20 pm, 7.50 pm, 8.25 pm, 8.40 pm.

W.J.Ponnington[?]
Brig. Gen, 102 Bde Dze[?]

31/7/16

38

ATHARVA
Vol 3

Army Form C. 2118

WAR DIARY
or
INTELLIGENCE SUMMARY
(Erase heading not required.)

Instructions regarding War Diaries and Intelligence Summaries are contained in F. S. Regs., Part II. and the Staff Manual respectively. Title Pages will be prepared in manuscript.

Place	Date	Hour	Summary of Events and Information	Remarks and references to Appendices
GIVENCHY SECTOR	MARCH 3.3	3.15 pm	Retaliation for bombardment.	I
			Wire cutting at A 96-4282	II
	6th	12 noon	Covering T.M. Batteries on Northern Crater	IIA
	6th-7th	1.30 am	Wire cutting	
	6th-7th mar-	mid-night	Bombardment in connection with blowing up a mine.	III
	11th	9 am	Covering T.M. Battery	IV
	14th	9 pm & 12 mn	Bombardment German reliefs.	V
	15th	12 noon	Covering T.M. Battery	VI
	18th	6 pm	Covering T.M. Battery	VII
	29th	4 am	Bombarding German horse transport	VIII

J. Mingleyford
Lt Col. B Goundee
38 C.R. Div?
31.3.16

Army Form C. 2118

WAR DIARY
or
INTELLIGENCE SUMMARY
(Erase heading not required.)

121st Brigade R.F.A.

Place	Date	Hour	Summary of Events and Information	Remarks and references to Appendices
	8/3/16		On the 8th March 1916 "J" Battery R.H.A. relieved "N" Battery R.H.A. and was attached to "B" Group R.F.A.	
	14th		Major H. Wilson Irwin R.F.A. having joined this Brigade from the 4th Division (R.A.6.) for duty on the 14th March 1916, was posted to command the 2nd Amm Column accordingly.	
	14th		The following transfers of Officers took place during the month:— 2nd Lt S.J. Rimmington from "A" Battery to 2nd Amm Column draft S.H. Rimmer dated 19th March 1916. 2nd Lt H. Rimmer from 2nd Amm Column to "H" Battery dated 14th March 1916. 2nd Lt Kyn Williams was transferred from the 2nd Amm Column to the Royal Flying Corps, dated 14th March 1916.	

Army Form C. 2118

WAR DIARY
or
INTELLIGENCE SUMMARY
(Erase heading not required.)

Appendix I

Place	Date	Hour	Summary of Events and Information	Remarks and references to Appendices
	1/3/16		Retaliation will be carried out tonight (1-2nd march) as follows:-	
			R.122. 1 X House at A11C 7/2.3½	
			2 X's Farm buildings A.5.d.04 (Strong farm)	
			1 salvo followed by 1 round G.F. at 2 am and again at 2.10 am	
			A/121. 1 X House at A.4.C.5.3	
			1 X Sweep A.4.C 3/2 3/2 to A.4.C.1.8 with H.E.	
			Both at 2 am. 1 salvo followed by 2 rounds G.F. and again at 2.15 am.	
			B.121. 2 x's at group of houses about A.10.d.10-7.-8	
			1 salvo followed by 2 rounds G.F with H E at 2 am and again at 2.15 am.	
			D.121. 2 x's A.4.C.6.2. — A.4.a. 1/2.0	
			1 X A.4.C 1/2.9 1/2 (Houses) with HE	
			Both 1 salvo followed by 2 rounds G.F at 2 am and again at 2.15 Am.	
			D.120. 3 Guns on VIOLAINES X roads A.S.A. 5/2.9.	
			1 salvo followed by 2 rounds G.F at 2 am and again at 2.10 am	

Army Form C. 2118

APPENDIX II

WAR DIARY
or
INTELLIGENCE SUMMARY
(Erase heading not required.)

Place	Date	Hour	Summary of Events and Information	Remarks and references to Appendices
	2/3/16		The following scheme will be carried out on 3rd March at 12 noon. Light & medium T.M. Batteries will open fire on the east edge of the Northern craters at 12 noon. The 2" Mortars (60 pdrs) will open fire on the same place at 1 section A/122 will open fire in conjunction with 2" M's at trench junctions A.9.b. 4½.2. at 12-1 pm. 1 section A/122 will fire at trench junctions H.9.b. 6½.1½. - A.9.b. 4½.4. Ammunition 75 rounds H.E. 1 Section A/121 barrage AUSTRIAN WAY (section fire 30 secs) 1 Gun B/121 Enfilade N. Edge of Salient A.9.b. 2½.4 - A.9.b. 6½.1½. (Section fire 1 minute) Fire will be maintained for 20 minutes.	
	3/3/16		N Bty R.H.A. will cut wire about A.9.b 4½.8½. between 2 pm and 3.15 pm today. From 3.15 pm to 31st day A/122 will fire 30 rounds H.E. at the parapet immediately behind the gap. From 3.45 pm - 4 pm A/121 will also fire 30 rounds H.E. at the same spot. The Best O.P. is W. House LE-PLANTIN. belonging to B/121	

WAR DIARY
or
INTELLIGENCE SUMMARY
(Erase heading not required.)

Army Form C. 2118

Instructions regarding War Diaries and Intelligence Summaries are contained in F.S. Regs., Part II. and the Staff Manual respectively. Title Pages will be prepared in manuscript.

Appendix III

Place	Date	Hour	Summary of Events and Information	Remarks and references to Appendices
	6/3/16		At midnight tonight 6th-7th. a mine will be sprung at northern edge of minefield opposite DUCK'S BILL. Every inducement, such as rockets, cheers, bombs, smoke bombs &c will be given to the Germans to man their parapets. The artillery programme will be as follows:-	
		1.30 pm	6th March 1.30 pm N.R.H.A. will cut wire extending existing gap, between SAXON WAY and A.9.a.84. 125 rds Shrapnel + 25 rds H.E. may be expended.	
		3 pm	B/122 will fire 30 rounds at parapet immediately behind point where fresh mine is cut i.e. about A.9.d.8½.4½.	
	7.3.16	12-1 am to 12-3 am	B/121 Barrage support line A.16.a.b.8½ – A.10.c.2.b. A.10.c.½.b. – A.9.b.6.1. A 121 " " Lines open cut and sweep. 1 salvo each followed by seven fire 20 secs.	

WAR DIARY
INTELLIGENCE SUMMARY

Army Form C. 2118

Appendix III

Place	Date	Hour	Summary of Events and Information	Remarks and references to Appendices
	9/3/14	12.5 to 12.40am	B/121 & A/121 left to Reserve Trench on same zone at XF 30 secs.	
		12.30am	1 × B/120 search front line from A.9.c.4½.0. – A.9.a.8.5. 1 × " Support line " = A.9.a.8h.9. – A.10.c.4½.2½. × F 15 secs for ½ minute.	
		12.36am	1 × B/120 remains on front trench 1 × B/120 Reserve trench A.10.C.4½.1½. – A.10.C.4½. 2½. × F 15 secs for ½ minute.	
			During this time 12.1 – 12.4 am 1 × B/122 Trench S = A.10 C. 4½. 2½ 1 × B/122 " = A.10.C. ½. 6. – A.10.C.2.b × F 30 secs. 1 × B.122 & B/121 will stand by for retaliation from Northern Salient (A.9.b).	

Army Form C. 2118

Appendix V

WAR DIARY
or
INTELLIGENCE SUMMARY
(Erase heading not required.)

Place	Date	Hour	Summary of Events and Information	Remarks and references to Appendices
	14/3/16	8pm	The following scheme will be carried out tonight 14th March.	
			H.156	
			1 Section Track A.17.a.5.1. – A.12.b.6.2½.	
			" " A.16.d.4½.6. – A.12.c.3.5.	
			" 1 salvo followed by 2 rounds gun fire	
		9pm	B.121 2 Sections A.11.c.8.4. – A.11.a.8.2.	
			1 salvo followed by 2 rounds gun fire	
		9.pm	A.121, 1 section A.10.d.1.8. – A.10.a.2½.8½.	
			" A.10.a.2.1. – A.10.a.9.0 (CANTELEUX ALLEY N).	
			" 1 salvo followed by 2 rounds gun fire	
		9pm	R.121 1 section A.4.d.0½. – A.10.b.7.9 (TRAMWAY).	
			1 salvo followed by 2 rounds gun fire.	
			From 12 midnight to 12.30 am. Batteries will fire salvos at	
			irregular averaging 5 min. at same targets.	
			In addition	
			R/120 1 section A.10.b.9½.8½. – A.11.a.4.5.	
			1 section Reserve Trench A.10.A.1½.½. – A.10.c.6.6.	
			S.R.O.G. " deliver averaging 5 min intervals	

Army Form C. 2118

Appendix IV

WAR DIARY
or
INTELLIGENCE SUMMARY
(Erase heading not required.)

Place	Date	Hour	Summary of Events and Information	Remarks and references to Appendices
	11/3/16	9 am	T.M. Battery no 61 will fire 10 rounds at A.9.b. 4½.0 at 9 am 11th March '16.	

1 X A/122 tm t ire trench at A.9.b 4½.2 to A.9.b. 4½.4 in conjunction with trench stms.

1 X. trench gns A.9.b 6½.3. + A.9.b 6½.5.

X g. 1 min for 2 o min from 9 am.

1 X A/121 enfilade AUSTRIAN WAY.
1 X " " PRUSSIAN WAY
XF 1+5 secs for 20 mins from 9 am

9.20 1X search support trench A.9.b. 4½.4½. to A.9.a. 8½.9. at
XF 30 secs from 9am to 9.20 am.
German Reserve trench A.9.b. 9.4 — A.10.a. 2.1.
XF 15 secs from 9.5 to 9.6 am

from 9.10 am — 9.12 am Reserve trench A.10.a. 1½.½. — A.10.c. 4½.7½.
XF 15 secs

from 9.14 am — 9.16 am Support trench A.10.c. 2.6. — A.10.a.5.½
XF 15 secs

from 9.15 — 9.20 Reserve trench A.9.b. 9.4. — A.10.A. 2.1.
XF 15 secs.

Army Form C. 2118

WAR DIARY
or
INTELLIGENCE SUMMARY

(Erase heading not required.)

Appendix VI

Instructions regarding War Diaries and Intelligence Summaries are contained in F.S. Regs., Part II. and the Staff Manual respectively. Title Pages will be prepared in manuscript.

Place	Date	Hour	Summary of Events and Information	Remarks and references to Appendices
	15/3/16		The following scheme will be carried out in conjunction with French troops to-day at 12 noon to 12.20pm on Rifle Bill. French troops will fire 10 rounds timed in conjunction with 1 section of F/122.	
			1st hour of this section will fire on A.10.C. 1/2.5. + A.10.C ½.2/2	
			1 section Stores Hill fire on A.10.C.3 3/2 + A.10.C.5.1	
			1 " A/121 will search SAXON WAY	
			1 " D/121 will search support trench from A.10.C.2.6 - A.10.C.5.D.	
			1 " B/121 " " communication trench from.	
			A.10.C.2.1/2 - A.10.C.5.1.	
			Rate of fire - 18 rds Sections fire 45 secs for 20mm Starting at 12 noon	
			F/122 1 section as arranged in conjunction with French troops.	
			1 " 2nd section fire 1 minute for 1 minute for 20 minutes	

Appendix VII

Date	Hour	Summary of Events and Information	Remarks and references to Appendices
18/3/16		The following scheme will be carried out tomorrow 19/3/16 from 6 a.m. to 6.20 a.m. The 2" T.H Battery will fire at the back of the Northern Crater, to destroy snipers posts and a M.G. Emplacements there. The following Artillery programme will take place from 6 a.m. to 6.20 a.m. R/122 will fire in conjunction with the French slows targets, Trench Junctions A.9.b. 4½. 1½ - A.9.a. 8.5. fire 1 min (20 rounds) 1 Gun Support trench A.9.b. 5. 3½ A.9.a. 8½. 5. 2 min interval (10 rounds).	

Army Form C. 2118

WAR DIARY
or
INTELLIGENCE SUMMARY
(Erase heading not required.)

124/RFA
Vol. 4

Place	Date	Hour	Summary of Events and Information	Remarks and references to Appendices
	5/6		2nd Lieut M. L. Remington with 1 NCO and 2 Gunners proceeded to undergo a course of instruction at the Trench Mortar school ST VENANT.	
	8th		The following Officers proceeded on leave during the month for 10 days. Captain A. G. Stephenson Lt Colonel N. G. Pringle Captain Y. E. Marston.	
	22nd			
	28th		The undermentioned Officers were attached to 122nd Bde RFA	
	26th		2nd Lieut R.A. Morgan 2nd Lieut C. A. Anydoea-Saundels.	

HJSS Hood
Major OC
Comdg 124 Bde

WAR DIARY
or
INTELLIGENCE SUMMARY

(Erase heading not required.)

Army Form C. 2118

Appendix VIII

Place	Date	Hour	Summary of Events and Information	Remarks and references to Appendices
	30/3/16		The Germans are using the road between A.4.C.4.1 and A.10.C.5.8 for Horse transport in the early morning. To discourage this the following programme will be carried tomorrow march 20.3.16.	
		4 am	R/120 2 rds S.F. on A.4.C.4.1. — A.10.a.5.8 R.121 1 sectn 2 rds S.F. on C4th ST ROCH. Cross Roads.	

J M Murphy (?) Lt Col
O/C B Group R.A.
38th Divn

31.3.16

Army Form C. 2118

WAR DIARY
or
INTELLIGENCE SUMMARY
(Erase heading not required.)

Instructions regarding War Diaries and Intelligence Summaries are contained in F. S. Regs, Part II. and the Staff Manual respectively. Title Pages will be prepared in manuscript.

Place	Date	Hour	Summary of Events and Information	Remarks and references to Appendices
	16/4/16		On the 16th April the Brigade went into rest with the exception of 'C' Battery who still remained in action. Considerable difficulty was found in obtaining a Billet for the Headquarters of the Brigade and the following morning moves took place.	
	17/4/16		On the 17th the Brigade Headquarters received orders from R.A. Headquarters, 38th Division to vacate the Billets moved into on the 16th – as we were in the 19th Divisional area, we therefore had no option but to proceed to another Billet which we were able to remain in until 23rd instns having been issued again on 22nd from R.A. Headqrs to vacate these as we were in Billets allotted to 19th Division.	
	22/4/16			
	23rd		We moved to another Billet on the 23rd and had to vacate this one owing to being in the area of the Australian Corps.	

WAR DIARY
or
INTELLIGENCE SUMMARY
(Erase heading not required.)

Army Form C. 2118

Place	Date	Hour	Summary of Events and Information	Remarks and references to Appendices
	1/4/16	6 a.m.	Our Artillery fired on the enemy trenches with excellent results. The enemy retaliated but little or no damage was done.	
	1/4/16		In conjunction with the Trench Mortars we heavily bombarded the enemy line about Duck's Bill and the craters. The shooting was very accurate and much damage to enemy was reported. Very careful observation had been made.	

Army Form C. 2118

XXXVI / 121. R.F.A
Vol. 5

WAR DIARY
or
INTELLIGENCE SUMMARY

(Erase heading not required.)

Instructions regarding War Diaries and Intelligence Summaries are contained in F.S. Regs., Part II. and the Staff Manual respectively. Title Pages will be prepared in manuscript.

Place	Date	Hour	Summary of Events and Information	Remarks and references to Appendices
	1/5/16		With the exception of C and D Batteries 121 Brigade R.F.A the Brigade still remained in rest. C & D Batteries were with the Left Group under Lt Col Patterson.	
	6/5/16		On this date the Brigade Commander (Lt Colonel N.S. Pringle R.F.A.) took over command of the XI Corps Artillery training Area at LAMBRES. N° AIRE, and 'A' Battery 121 Brigade proceeded to LAMBRES for training and remained there for one week, i.e. 13/5/16. 'B' Battery were the next Battery to go into training at LAMBRES. This Battery also underwent one week's training returning their Billets on 20/5/16. Though this training was rather severe, undoubtedly the mentioned Batteries became far more efficient as regards their qualifications in Battery movements.	
	13/5/16			

WAR DIARY
or
INTELLIGENCE SUMMARY

Army Form C. 2118

(Erase heading not required.)

Place	Date	Hour	Summary of Events and Information	Remarks and references to Appendices
	21/5/16		Owing to the reorganization of D.A.C. all Brigade Ammunition Columns, subsequently Ammunition was received direct from D.A.C. instead of B.A.C.	
	29/5/16		On this date A/121 relieved C/119 who were in action at Point M.5 b 0.8.	
	29/5/16		Under the scheme for the reorganization of the Divl Arty the following Batteries changed their nomenclature to form complete Brigades. C/121 became C/122 A/121 " C/121 A/122(How) " B/121	
	30/5/16 3/5/16		These changes took effect from 12 noon 24th May 1916. B/121 relieved C/120th who were in action at M.15. A.5.5.	

Commanding :-
121st Brigade, R.F.A.
Lieut-Colonel, R.A.
E. Cobbe

XXXVIII

121st Bde. R.F.A.

Army Form C. 2118

WAR DIARY
or
INTELLIGENCE SUMMARY
(Erase heading not required.)

Instructions regarding War Diaries and Intelligence Summaries are contained in F.S. Regs., Part II. and the Staff Manual respectively. Title Pages will be prepared in manuscript.

Place	Date	Hour	Summary of Events and Information	Remarks and references to Appendices
In the field.	June 1916			
	11th		Between these dates there is nothing to report. 121 Brigade Headquarters who were in training at LAMBRES returned to LA-BASSEE ROAD to rejoin the Brigade.	
	12th		A/121 and C/121 coming out of action joined Brigade Headquarters and proceeded to LE-SART	
	13th		Units mentioned on the 12th moved from their billets in LE-SART via LILLERS for the purpose of proceeding to DIVION resting there for one night. "A/122 and "B/122 came under O.C. 121st Brigade R.F.A. for the march.	
	14th		After passing the night at DIVION units moved off together to BERLES. "A/121 and "C/121 were ordered into action and were attached to the 51st Division.	

Army Form C. 2118

121 Bde R.F.A.

WAR DIARY
or
INTELLIGENCE SUMMARY
(Erase heading not required.)

Instructions regarding War Diaries and Intelligence Summaries are contained in F.S. Regs., Part II. and the Staff Manual respectively. Title Pages will be prepared in manuscript.

Place	Date	Hour	Summary of Events and Information	Remarks and references to Appendices
	17th		121 Brigade Headquarters marched to GRAND CAMP where they joined B/121 and D/121 who came out of action on the 14th (and marched with another group). to GRAND CAMP, and underwent with 121 Brigade Headquarters 10 days training.	
	27th		On this date training finished, 121st Brigade Headquarters B/121 and D/121 vacated training area and proceeded to HEUZECOURT. A/120th were attached to 121st Brigade for this march, which was made by night, units arriving at destination on morning of 28th.	

J.M. Murphy Major
OC 121 Brigade R.F.A.

1875 Wt. W593/826 1,000,000 4/15 J.B.C. & A. A.D.S.S./Forms/C. 2118.

38th Div.
XV.Corps.

Division transferred
from II.Corps, Fourth
Army, 3.7.16.

Headquarters,

121st BRIGADE, R.F.A.

J U L Y

1916

Attached:

Appendices 1, 2, 3,
4 & 5.

Army Form C. 2118

WAR DIARY
INTELLIGENCE SUMMARY
(Erase heading not required.)

CXXI. RFA
JULY.

Place	Date	Hour	Summary of Events and Information	Remarks and references to Appendices
	1916 JULY 1st.		The 121st Brigade R.F.A. moved off from HEUZECOURT at 6 p.m. and marched to MIRVAUX arriving at 1.10 a.m. At 11 P.m. night of 1st/2nd, Brigade proceeded to HARPONVILLE and reached its destination at 3.30 a.m. on morning	
	2nd.		of 2nd and rested at HARPONVILLE for one day.	
	3rd. 5th.		From there Brigade moved off at 6.45 p.m. for Camp at TREUX WOODS arriving there at 5.10 a.m. on morning of the 4th and rested there until 7 p.m. on the evening of the 5th when the Brigade marched to FRICOURT arriving at 3.20 a.m. on morning of the 6th, Batteries moving straight into action, being temporarily attached to 21st Division.	
	6/7th		All lines of fire were immediately laid out on MAMETZ WOOD. On night of 6/7th the 52nd Brigade attacked PEARL ALLEY, QUADRANGLE SUPPORT & QUADRANGLE ALLEY. Attack commenced at 2 a.m. and was preceded by a General Bombardment of 121st Brigade in conjunction with 79th Brigade (appendix 1)	
	7th.		The above attack failed. Orders were received during the day that the Infantry would attack QUADRANGLE SUPPORT TRENCH to Junction with PEARL ALLEY - ACID DROP COPSE - STRIP of WOOD between WOOD TRENCH and WOOD SUPPORT, at 8 p.m. One 18 pdr. was turned on LOST COPSE One 18 pdr on FRONT EDGE of WOOD (X.23.b.5.8.) to (X.18.a.8.4.) One 4.5" Howitzer on PEARL ALLEY (appendix 2.)	
	8th.		During the day 18 pdr. Batteries fired on MAMETZ WOOD. F.O.O. reported German Infantry advancing from PEARL ALLEY down communication trench towards MAMETZ WOOD. C/121 were ordered to turn their fire on to N.W. corner of MAMETZ WOOD for 20 minutes at section fire 20 seconds. D/121 to fire 40 rounds on PEARL WOOD.	
	9th.		On this date 21st Div. Arty. instructed that the following task had been allotted to this Brigade : Shell LOST COPSE X.17.d.9.8. and PEARL WOOD from 7 a.m. until further orders. Night firing was carried out on MAMETZ WOOD. (Appendix 3)	
	10th /11th		During the day PEARL ALLEY X.17.c.8.5. the CUTTING was searched. Rate of fire - Section fire 30 seconds. A scheme was arranged to engage targets allotted in para 8. of 21st D.A. Operation Order (attached)	4

Army Form C. 2118

WAR DIARY
or
INTELLIGENCE SUMMARY

(Erase heading not required.)

Instructions regarding War Diaries and Intelligence Summaries are contained in F. S. Regs., Part II. and the Staff Manual respectively. Title Pages will be prepared in manuscript.

Place	Date	Hour	Summary of Events and Information	Remarks and references to Appendices
	10th/11th contd.		On the night 10/11th "B", "C" & "D" Batteries moved and took up a forward position, C/121 to position 1,000 yards South of MAMETZ WOOD, "B"=121 to QUEENS NULLAH, D/121 on left of B/121.	
	12th.		B/121 and C/121 bombarded German front line on their respective zones. (Map attached) The Support line of whole Brigade zone was shelled by A/121.(howitzer) The front line over whole of Brigade zone was shelled by D/121(Howitzer) (Appendix 6.) Information was received at 5.15 p.m. that the Germans were advancing over Crest towards MAMETZ WOOD. An order was given to B/121 to fire on to front of BAZENTIN WOOD and increase rate of fire to section fire 20 seconds and keep this up till 7 p.m.	(5)
	13th/14th		Morning 13/14th attack was made by our Infantry on HIGH WOOD (Appendix 7) The enemy put up a barrage on Southern portion of BAZENTIN-le-PETIT WOOD 8 a.m. Our Cavalry received orders to push through between the two WOODS (BAZENTIN-le-GRAND & MAMETZ) and orders were issued that unless Observers can see the situation, all fire must be kept North of the new trench from M.33.c. through HIGH WOOD to S.6.d.	
	15th/16th		8.30 a.m. to 9 a.m. a bombardment was carried out on Trench from S.2.b.3½.8. to end of trench S.2.a.7.5. Rate of fire 18 pdr. Section fire 20 seconds.	
	16th/17th		Orders were received to keep MARTINPUICH and German switch trench under continuous fire during night 16/17th. Rate of Fire 150 rounds per Brigade per hour. Brigade Headquarters moved forward to HIDDEN WOOD.	
	18th		An unconfirmed report was received from 21sr Divl. Headquarters at 12.55 p.m. that Germans were seen digging in, in S. 2 & 3. in front of Switch trench. F.O.O's received orders to stop this work, if seen.B/121 had orders to move into forward position near ACID DROP COPSE. this was carried out the same evening. Orders were received about 5 p.m. that the 121st Brigade were to move out of action and proceed to TREUX WOOD and arriving in following order -	
	19th		D/121 - 12.30 a.m., B/121 - 2 a.m.,C/121 - 3.30 a.m., A/121 - 3.45 a.m.,Headquarters/121 = 11.30 a.m.at 4.15 P.m. Brigade marched to COIGNEUX arriving there at 2 a.m. on the 20th	

Army Form C. 2118

WAR DIARY
or
INTELLIGENCE SUMMARY
(Erase heading not required.)

- 3 -   Summary of Events and Information

Place	Date	Hour	Summary of Events and Information	Remarks and references to Appendices
	20th to 23rd.		Batteries of 121st Brigade then moved into action relieving the 240th Brigade forming part of LEFT GROUP commanded by Lieut-Col. RUDKIN D.S.O. Brigade Headquarters remaining in rest at COIGNEUX remaining at this village for 3 days. (J.18.c.5.0.)	
	24th,		At 9 a.m, Brigade Headquarters moved to (LEFT GROUP HEADQUARTERS) when Lieut-Col. H.G.PRINGLE R.F.A. took over command of LEFT GROUP on morning of this date, GROUP consisted of A/121, B, C & D batteries, and A.B.C & D batteries of 22nd Brigade R.F.A. On night of 24/25th B/122 and C/122 were ordered to move out of action and join the RIGHT GROUP.	
	24th/31st.		Trench Warfare took place. By night Batteries shelled exits to PUISIEUX to stop enemy's transport. By day Enemy Trench Mortars and Machine guns fired on.	

J.M.Brough Lt.Col.
Cmdg 121.M.Bde R.F.A

1/8/16

OPERATION ORDER.

1. The 52nd Brigade will tonight attack PEARL ALLEY QUADRANGLE SUPPORT and QUADRANGLE ALLEY X.22.b.6.8. - X.17.c.5.1. - X.23.c.5.6. Attack will commence at 2 a.m. and will preceedef by general bombardment.

2. "A"/121 will barrage line X.15.d.8½.7. - X.17.a.6.6. and sweep the line X.16.b.4.0. - X.16.b.8.4.
"C"/121 will barrage line X.16.d.7.3. - X.16.d.10.9. and sweep to line X.16.d. central X.16.b.7.1. - X.16.d.7.9.
"B"/121 will bombard CEMETARY X.17. c.8.0. (due South ACID DROP COPSE)
This bombardment will commence at 1.29 a.m. and be continued at Section fire 20 seconds till 1.55 a.m. when rate will be increased to Section fire 10 secdonds till 2.a.m.

3. From 2. a.m. to 2.30 a.m. barrage will be established in which "B"/121 will co-operate. Barrage will consist of one salvo followed by one round gun fire at intervals of 2 minutes. Targets X.16.d.7.3. to X.17.c.5.4. "B"/121 will be prepared to continue barrage longer if required.

4. "A"/121 and "C"/121 during preliminary bombardment will fire ½ H.E. and ½ Shrapnel.

5. Night firing will be continued, as ordered, previous and subsequent to bombardment

6. A further bombardment will commence at 7.20 a.m. 7th inst. Details will issued later.

7. Batteries should indent on 21st D.A.C. for ammunition to be at there Wagon Line in time to be delivered to the batteries by 6.a.m, on the 7th July in addition to anything already asked for.

6th July 1916.

Adj. 121st Bde R.F.A

2

(para 2 (a)) which will be maintained till 8.30 a.m

8.30-8.50am
 (c) After 8.30 am the programme of bombardment A will be continued but times will be as follows.

8.50-9.30am
 C Battery 1st Lift (para 2 c) will commence at 8.50 am and continue till 9.30 am.

9.30-10 am
 Lift ordered for C.B. and 1 section D Battery (para 2 d) will take place from 9.30 am 10 am.

 C Battery cease firing at 10 am
 Remainder continue to bombard PEARL WOOD as in para 2 c.

4. The portions of the Wood allotted will be thoroughly searched 80% H.E. will be fired by 18 pdrs.

G.D.Thomas Lt
Adj 12th Bde RFA

7-7-1916.

APPENDIX (3)

OPERATION ORDER.

Area for tonight firing JULY 9 / 10th

Following areas of MAMETZ WOOD allotted to 121st Brigde will now be considered permanent for night firing.

"C"/121   Southern limit as for last night
Northern limit K.18.c.9½.2. - K.17.d.7.6.

"B"/121   From above line to a line from North West Corner (X.18.a.1½. to S.13.d.2.8.

"A"/121   Area X.18.a.1½.8. - X.18.a.7.4. - S.13.b.2.9. - S.13.b.7.6. S.13.d.2.8.

"B"/121   As for last night but with addition of area shown RED on map

Ammunition :-

"A" Battery	140
"B" "	140
"C" "	140
"D" "	~~140~~ 80

In addition to above the following programme will be carried out Searching fire will be directed on the MACHINE GUN EMPLACEMENTS situated (1) on east edge of ACID DROP COPSE and (2) at Junction of QUADRANGLE ALLEY - MAMETZ WOOD.

The first target will engaged by "A" Battery and 2 Hows of "D" Battery.
Fire will be as follows :- 10.15 p.m. Section fire 20 secs for 10 mins. (Single How at 20 secs intervals in all cases.
10.45. p.m. Section fire 20 secs for 10 mins.
11.15 p.m. Section fire 20 secs for 15 mins.
At least 50% H.E. should be used by 18 pdrs.

9-7-1916.

G. Thomas Lieut.
Adj 121st Bde RFA

OPERATION ORDER   APPENDIX (4)

Reference attached order No 27, (1)   Task of 121st Brigade is to engage targets allotted in paragraph 8 from 3.30 a.m. to 8.15 a.m. and later unless orders are received to stop.

Target "A"/121   PEARL WOOD (Pearl Wood)
"   "B"/121   LOWER WOOD (Lower Wood)
"C" and "D"/121 DEAD PEARL ALLEY (Dead Pearl Alley) from X.17.c.8.5. to the Cutting in X.11.d.7.0½.

There must no fire West of a North and South line through ACID DROP COPSE.

The last two batteries "C" and "D" will commence with the portion of PEARL ALLEY lying between X.17.c.8.5. and the Cutting they will engage exclusively till 7.45 a.m. when they will lift on the Northern portion.

No Infantry movement is intended on the area crossed by our fire, but F.O.O. must be prepared to lift the fire back as far as the German lines, should they see our Infantry getting dangerously near to our own fire and take any advantage, and the retirement of the Germans in which case "A" and "B" batteries would lift on the in the first case to VILLN WOOD and PEARL WOOD.

RATE OF FIRE.

3.30 a.m. to 4.15 a.m. Battery Fire 10 seconds

4.10 a.m. to 4.15 a.m.   "   "   5 seconds

4.15 a.m. to 4.20 a.m.   "   "   10 seconds

4.20 a.m. to 4.30 a.m.   "   "   15 seconds

4.30 a.m. onwards   "   "   20 seconds.

About half (½) H.E. should be used,

10-7-1916.

Appendix (2)

OPERATION ORDER

Reference MONTAUBAN SHEET
and Special Map

1. MAMETZ WOOD will be attacked by the 17th and 38th Divisions at 8 a.m. today 7th.
   At the same time 111rd Corps attack CONTALMAISON,
   Copy of 21st D.A. order is attached.
2. Task of the 121st Brigade will be as under

Bombardment A   A. "B" Battery   Small COPSE at S.17.d.8.9.(LOST COPSE)
7.20 - 7.52 am   1 section "D"   (shown on attached map)
7.52 - 8.a.m.   Battery.
   (B) A Battery   )
       1 Section D) PEARL WOOD (X.17.b.9.8.)
       Battery   )

   "C" Battery   Search and sweep portion of MAMETZ WOOD
                 X.18.c.5.4. - X.18.c.9.2. - S.13.b.1½.1½. -
                 X.18.a.9.2½. - X.18.c.5.4.

   Rate of fire
     7.20 - 7.52 am Section fire 20 seconds
     7.52 - 8. a.m.   "   " 10 "

8.0am - 8.20 am
   B.   Same Targets.

   Rate of fire Section fire 20 secs.

C/121 1st Lift
8.20am-9 am (C) "C" Battery will lift to position of their target lying
             North of the line X.18.c.6.6.
             Remainder same targets
             Rate Section fire 20 seconds

C/121 2nd lift(D) "C" Battery will lift to thaxix portion of their targets
B/121 1st lift.   North of an East and West line running through S.13 cent AA.
½ D121 "   "B" Battery and the section of "D" Battery lift to
9. - 9.30am   PEARL WOOD (S.17.b.9.8.
             Rate of fire Section fire 30 seconds.

9.30 a.m.   (E) "A","B" and "D" batteries continue on PEARL WOOD
             Rate of fire Section Fire 40 seconds
             "C" Battery cease firing.

Bombardment "B"
   3. (a) If the operation detailed in Operation order No 19
      tonight, is not successful the bombardment carried out
7.20-8.am   under that order will be repeated from 7.20 am -8.am.
8- 8-30am (b) At 8 am all guns will lift to bombardment A will

APPENDIX (5)

No.574.

Reference 1/20,000 MONTAUBAN & XV Corps Special 2nd Line Map, attached

1. A bombardment will take place on morning of "Z" day (13th inst.) minutes before zero (time to be notified later)

2. Up to this hour, night firing will be carried on as usual

3. Tasks for bombardment will be as in table "A".

4. Heavy Artillery will co-operate by shelling front and support lines.

5. The assault will take place at zero time. The advance of the infantry will be supported by successive barrages; Tasks &c are shown in Table "B".

6. Counter-battery work will be undertaken by the Heavy Artillery and will start 10 minutes before the bombardment begins and will continue as required.

7. There is no restriction as to expenditure of ammunition of 18 pounders or 4.5 Howitzer ammunition.

8. It will be necessary to push batteries forward as quickly as possible to support the infantry when they have gained their objective.
   The 95th, 78th & 79th brigades will be prepared to send forward batteries to support the infantry as soon as the infantry have reached their objective.

9. Acknowledge

D. PAGE   Capt. R.H.A.

11th July, 1916.   Brigade-Major, 21st Divisional Artillery.

TABLE "B"

BARRAGES.

BARRAGE "A" (Blue Line)   0. to 1 hour and 1.15 to 1.45.

At Zero. All Howitzers will lift on to the line just in front of the Support Line direct, and 18-pr batteries will search back by lifts of 50 yards to the Support Line. Guns will be told off to search back along the communication trenches.   At the same time the batteries which have been firing on the Support Line up to Zero will search back slowly through the Wood and Village in their respective zones. These batteries will continue to search forwards and backwards behind the barrage, until the final barrage has been reached.

BARRAGE "B" (Red Line) 1.0 to 1.15

Fire will remain on barrage "A" until 1 hour after zero when Guns and Howitzers will lift direct to the Red Line (S.8.d.1.1. to S.7.d.5.7.) No rounds to fall South of this line. An Infantry party will then cut the wire in front of Support Line and will return.   Guns and Howitzers will return to Barrage "A" at 1.15 and will continue to 1.45 and 1.40.

BARRAGE "B" (1.45 to 2.15)

At 1.40. 4.5 Howitzers will search back by 100 Yards to the Red line barrage "B".   Guns will leave Barrage "A" at 1.45 and will search back by increases in range of 50 Yards.

BARRAGE "C" (2.15 to 2.45)

At 2.15 Howitzers will search back by 100 yards to the Yellow Line. No shell to fall South of line (S.8.c.9.5.4 to S.7.d.0.9) and at 2.20 guns will search back by lifts of 50 yards.   During this Barrage the Wood north of the Yellow line will be searched continually by the guns.

BARRAGE "D" (2.45 to 3 hours 5 mins)

At 2.40 Howitzers will search back by 100 Yards at a time to the Green Line (S.8.c.9.7. to S.8.c.35.12) thence in a straight line to North West corner of the Wood (no rounds to fall SOUTH of this Line)   At 2.45 guns will search back by 50 yards at a time to the Green Line.   During this barrage special attention should be paid to the house at S.3.a.4.0.

TABLE "A"

Bombardments from :-

Front line trench and their respective zones will be engaged by "B" and "C" batteries.

Support line over whole Brigade zone will be shelled by "A"121

Front line over whole Brigade Zone will be shelled by "D" Battery.

Rate of Fire :-

All batteries will fire Section fire 15 seconds till at least 10 minutes when rate will be increased to as near section fire 5 seconds as possible.

BARRAGE "E" (3 Hrs 5 mins to 3.25)

At 3 hours after Zero, all Howitzers will search back to a line running from S.6.a.9.5. to N.E. Corner of Wood - along West end of village (Purple Line) by increases of 100 yards
At 3 hours 5 mins guns will proceed similarly (increases in range by 50 yards)

BARRAGE "F" 3.25 to 3.50.

At 3.20 Howitzers will search back to the line S.8.a.85.10 to N.E. corner of Wood along Western end of Village (Brown Line)
At 3.25 guns will search back by lifts of 50 yards.

BARRAGE "G"

At 3.50 Howitzers and at 3.55 all guns will search to the extreme North of the village when Howitzers will cease firing and the guns will form a defensive barrage.
As the advance proceeds, it will be necessary to form a defensive barrage on the Left Flank, probably entailing the employment of one brigade. Details of this barrage and the final
Flank   barrage will be issued later.
During barrages, fire will be at the rate of Section fire 20 seconds (or its equivalent) and for the 5 minutes before each lift it will be increased to Section fire 10 seconds
Heavy Guns will continue with Counter Battery work.

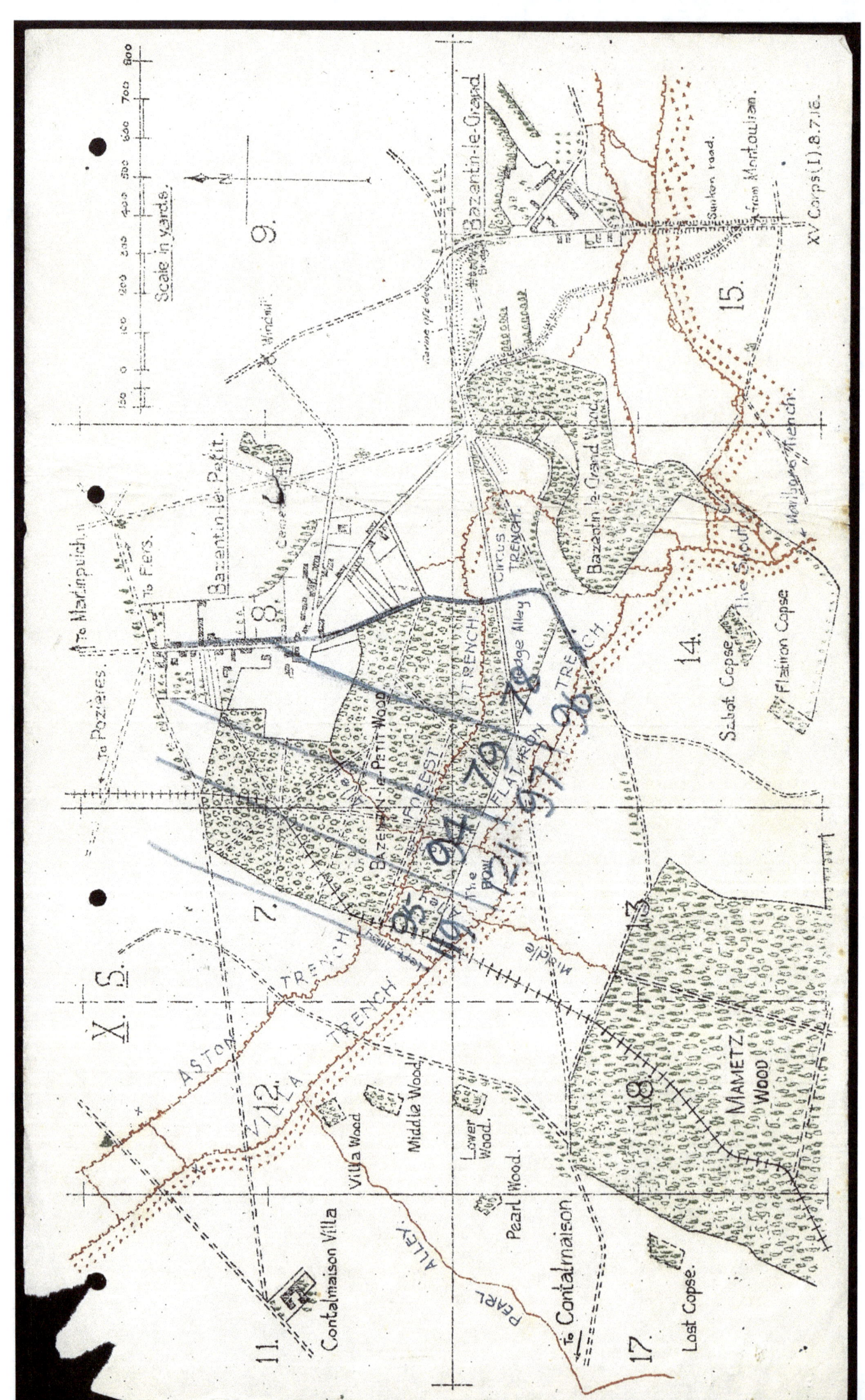

WAR DIARY or INTELLIGENCE SUMMARY

Army Form C. 2118

Place	Date	Hour	Summary of Events and Information	Remarks and references to Appendices
SAILLY-AU-BOIS	August 3rd	3 p.m.	Brigade was in action near HEBUTERNE. Wirecutting was carried out as per attached Operation order.	OPERATION ORDER No 2.
	4th – 6th		This was repeated during 4th, 5th & 6th, extending the area tackled about 100 yards North and South each day. On 6th C/121 cut wire near the HOOK (further South) while B/121 fired at wire over the whole area cut by them during the three previous days. Wirecutting on the whole effective, though the wire here is very thick.	
	6th 7th		On the nights 6th – 7th and 7th – 8th, Batteries of 121st Brigade R.F.A. (one section per night) was relieved by Batteries of Guards Divl. Arty. Guns were taken out of pits, proceeding thence to COIGNEUX.	
	7th		Bombardment of German Trenches carried out as per attached Arty. Programme. This was apparently successful in breaking the enemy's trenches. The enemy retaliated with Shell and Trench Mortar Bombs and much Machine gun fire for about ½ hour.	ARTILLERY PROGRAMME August 7 1916.
AUTHIE	8th		Brigade proceeded to AUTHIE, where it rested for 3 days.	
HEM - (DOULLENS)	11th		Brigade marched to HEM (near DOULLENS) where it stayed till night of 13th.	
ZEGGERS - CAPPEL	14th		The Brigade marched to CANDAS station and entrained at 5.50 a.m. for St. OMER, detraining here, the Brigade marched Northwards to ZEGGERS - CAPPEL resting for 10 days at this village.	

WAR DIARY
or
INTELLIGENCE SUMMARY

August 1916.

Army Form C. 2118

Place	Date	Hour	Summary of Events and Information	Remarks and references to Appendices
	6/7		More wirecutting.	D28
	7/8		Battery relieved by C/174 & Guard Division	D28
	8th		Marched to AUTHIE.	D4
	10th		" " HEM.	D4
	13th		Entrained CANDAS. Detrained ST OMER. Marched to ZEGGERS CAPPEL.	D4
	20th		Brigade sports. Dismounted Turn-out competition	D4
	21st		Lt GOOD transferred to Antiaircraft.	D4
	22nd		Relieved 127th & 135th S.S. of ELVERDINGHE.	D4
			Lt ELLIOT transferred to Guards Div. Trench mortars.	D4
	28th		Formed into 6-gun battery with 1 section of late A/120.	
	29th		28 Gunners and 67 N.C.O.'s and men taken on strength. Relieved by new A/121 (late A/120). Relieved C/122 just north of YPRES.	D4
			Officers with battery.	

Capt. D.C. Stephenson
Lieut. W.Q.C. Stone
2nd Lieut. J. Thompson
" F. Ripley

D.C. Stephenson
Comdg. C/121

WAR DIARY or INTELLIGENCE SUMMARY

Army Form C. 2118

Place	Date	Hour	Summary of Events and Information	Remarks and references to Appendices
YPRES.	20th 21st		Advantage was taken of this rest to organise Brigade Sports and a Brigade Concert, which proved very successful and aroused keen competition.	
	23rd		On 20th & 21st detachments entrained from ZEGGERS CAPPEL and went into action in the North of the YPRES Salient, relieving Units of the 4th Divl. Artillery. Wagon lines remained at ZEGGERS CAPPEL till Aug.23rd when the Brigade marched out at 3.30 a.m. and proceeded via WORMHOUDT and POPERINGHE to wagon lines of relieved Batteries North of POPERINGHE. Batteries of 121st Brigade now came under Colonel Commanding LEFT GROUP. The 121st Brigade 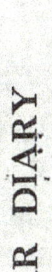 was located at PROVEN. HEADQUARTERS	
	25th		Guns brought by this Brigade to Wagon lines were handed over complete to Units of 3rd Canadian Divisional Artillery, with exception of 2 Guns of D/121. which were kept.	
	25th		Orders were received that the Brigade was to be re-constituted - 3 - 6 Gun 18 Pdr. Batteries and 1 - 4 gun 4.5" Howitzer Battery. A/121 was split up between B/121. and C/121, and a new battery (now called A/121.) added from 120th Brigade R.F.A. D/121. remains the same This reorganization took effect from 29th August.	
	29th			

S.Cooper MAJOR RFA.
COMMANDING - 121st BRIGADE RFA

ARTILLERY PROGRAMME - AUGUST 7th, 1916.

The following programme will be carried out today (7th) by the LEFT GROUP with the object of breaking the GERMAN trenches :-

6" Howitzers. will fire -

    5 rounds on the POINT
   15 ,, ,, ,, HOOK (K.23.b.6.0.)
   30 ,, ,, ,, 2nd Line from Junction of Trench and hedge, (K.24.a.0.2½.) to junction of road and trench (K.23.b.9½.3½.)

4.5" Howitzers.

    D/121 from Trench junction (K.24.c.1½.9½.) to Trench Junction K.24.a.1.1.   50 rounds.

    D/121 Front Line K.23.d.9.6. - K.23.d.9.8.   50 rounds.

    D/122 Front Line K.23.b.6.0. - K.23.b.5½.4.   100 rounds.

Stokes Mortars.

    Trench Mortar K.23.d.8.9½.
         ,,   K.23.b.6.3.

18-pdrs.

    A/121. C.T. K.23.b.6.0. - K.23.b.9½.3½.
    B/121. 2nd Line K.23.b.9½.3½. - K.23.b.8.6.
    C/121. Front Line K.23.d.9.8. - K.23.b.7.0.
    A/122. Front Line from Trench Junction K.23.d.8.3½. - K.23.d.9.6. (section fire 40 seconds all H.E)

Machine Guns.

    (a) 59th M.G. Coy. will fire on 3rd Line trench between K.24.c.8.5. and K.17.d.6.2.
    (b) 60th M.G. Coy. will co-operate by bursts of fire on hostile C.T's running -
        (a) from Front Line to STAR WOOD.
        (b) ,, ,, ,, ,, LA LOUVIERE FARM.

Times as under :-
    6" Hows.   4 p.m. - 5 p.m.
    4.5" & 18 pdrs.   5 p.m. - 6 p.m.
    Stokes Mortars.   5.15 p.m. - 6 p.m.
    M.G's (bursts of fire.) 4 p.m. - 6 p.m.

August 7th, 1916.

                                              2/Lieut. R.F.A.
                                    Adjutant LEFT GROUP R.F.A.

OPERATION ORDER No.2.

PROGRAMME FOR 3rd AUGUST, 1916.

---

3 p.m.   "B"/121   Fire 400 rounds at wire from the POINT to
                  TRENCH JUNCTION K.23.b.1.9½. "K" O.P. and
                  forward observing.

         "C"/121   Fire 400 rounds at wire just South of POINT
                  for 100 yards.
                  Of this the last 60 rounds should be H.E.
                  distributed along whole front damaged.

5 p.m.   "D"/121   Fire 100 rounds at parapet behind wire
                  engaged by "B"/121.

         "D"/122   Fire 100 rounds at Parapet behind wire
                  damaged by "C"/121.

         The above rounds are in addition to the daily
         allotment.

3rd August.

                                   C.T.Crozier   R.F.A.
                                   Commanding 121st Brigade R.F.A.

War Diary

B Battery, 121st Brigade R.F.A. period ending 31.8.16

Place	Date	Time		Appendices
ELVERDINGHE	Night 21/22 Aug 1916		B/121 Left Section relieved left section B/134th B/135 RFA in action about 600ˣ E of ELVERDINGHE VILLAGE	
	"		Right Section A/121 (attached to B/121) relieved right section 134th B/135 RFA in action in ELVERDINGHE VILLAGE.	
	Night 22/23 Aug 1916		Right Section B/121 relieved centre section 134th B/135 RFA in action about 800ˣ E of ELVERDINGHE VILLAGE	
	28.8.16.		Right Section A/121 absorbed as left section B/121 on orders being received. Orig. splitting up A/121 and orig. moving B/121 to six gun establishment. Left section B/121 to become centre section.	

J.K. Marston
O.C. B/121st Bde R.F.A.   Captain R.F.A.

WAR DIARY — D Battery 121 Brigade RFA
from August 22nd 1916 to 31st August 1916

Place	Date	Time	Target	No. of Rounds
	21-8-16	2 pm to 2.30 pm	Registration	8 rounds H.E.
	22-8-16 to 24-8-16	—	– NIL –	
	25-8-16	7-30 pm	Registration of PILCKEM MILL	10 rounds H.E.
	26-8-16	12-15 pm	Registration HINDENBURGH FARM	7 rounds
	– „ –	4-25 pm	KOLN FARM	12 – „ –
	– „ –	4-35 pm	PILCKEM MILL	18 – „ –
	– „ –	4-50 pm	CRAB APPLE TREE	7 – „ –
	– „ –	5-15 pm	HIGH COMMAND REDOUBT	6 – „ –
	27-8-16	—	– NIL –	
	28-8-16	2 pm	KOLN FARM. Registration	5 rounds H.E.
	29-8-16	6-45 pm	vicinity PILCKEM	10 rounds H.E.
		11-15 pm	on S.O.S. lines	20 „ H.E.
	30-8-16 to 31-8-16	—	– NIL –	

2-9-16.

C H Jones 2 Lt
for Commanding D/121 Bde RFA

SECRET   G.S. No. 838

38th DIVISIONAL ARTILLERY

DRAFT OPERATION ORDERS

1. In conjunction with operations on the 2nd Army front, the 38th Division will co-operate with wire cutting and a bombardment followed by a raid. The wire cutting and bombardment will last three days, the raid taking place on the night of the third day.
   This day ("Z" day) and Zero hour will be notified later.

2. The wire cutting will begin on "X" day and all arrangements for this will be complete by dawn on September 10th.

3. The Heavy Artillery VIIIth Corps will take part in the bombardments.

4. Group Commanders will arrange that during the concentrated bombardment they have sufficient guns which can be quickly turned on to any portion of their front.

5. During the nights "X"/"Y" and "Y"/"Z" the Infantry will arrange to fire at the gaps in the wire with Lewis guns and machine guns.

6. A C K N O W L E D G E

Issued at 11 p.m. September 8th 1916.

Geldard
Captain R.A.
Brigade Major, 38th Divisional Artillery.

Copies to:-

No. 1   R.A. VIIIth Corps
No. 2   38th Division "G"
No. 3   38th Division "Q"
No. 4 - 10 Right Group
No. 11-17 Left Group
No. 18   121st Brigade Headquarters
No. 19   Divl. Ammn. Column.

"X" DAY

Unit	Objective	No. of rounds	Time	Remarks
Right Group 18 pdrs.	Wirecutting C.15.c.9.8. C.14.b.6.3.	150 150	As Convenient	) All wire-) cutting will) be deliberate
Left Group 18 pdrs.	C.7.d.05.60. C.13.b.8.8. C.14.c.75.95. C.14.a.35.20.	150 250 250 250	" " " "	))))

"Y" DAY

Unit	Objective	No. of rounds	Time	Remarks
Right Group & Left Group 18 pdrs.	Wirecutting as for "X" Day	Same as "X" day	During morning	
Right Group 18 prs. & 4.5" Hows.	C.14.c.75.95. to C.14.b.6.3.	18 prs - 800 4.5 Hows - 300	Afternoon	)) Initial) bombardment on) front line and) support trenches)
Left Group 18 pdrs & 4.5" Hows.	C.13.b.8.8. 300rds to C.14.c.75.95.	18 prs - 1200 4.5" Hows - 300	"	
B/121	C.13.b.88 - C.14.a.1.7			
H.A. VIIIth Corps. 2-6" Hows.	C.13.b.8.8. to C.14.c.75.95. to C.14.b.6.3. HIGH COMMAND REDOUBT	100	"	))) Registration and) initial bombard-) ment on front) line and) support trenches)
2-60 prs.	FARM 14 FORTIN 17 KOLN FARM ESSEN FARM	100	"	

"Z" DAY

Unit	Objective	No. of rounds	Time	Remarks
Right and Left Group 18 pdrs	Wirecutting as necessary	?	Morning	Only sufficient rounds to re-open any gaps mended during night
Right Group 18 pdrs and 4.5" Hows.	Same as "Y" day	18 prs. - 2000 4.5" Hows- 600	} 2 Hours bombardment. Starting time will be notified later.	
Left Group 18 prs and 4.5" Hows.	-do- [B/121 750 rds.]	18 prs. - 3000 4.5" Hows- 800		
H.A. VIIIth Corps. 4 - 9.2" Hows	C.13.b.8.8. to C.14.c.75.95.	280		Heavy Bombardment
7 - 6" Hows.	C.14.c.75.95 to C.14.b.6.3. HIGH COMMAND REDOUBT	630		
8 - 4.7" guns	Enfilade face of Salient EOLIAN FARM	200		
4 - 60 prs.	as on "Y" day	200		

PROGRAMME FOR "Z" NIGHT

0 - 0.30.   Bombardment on same objectives as in the afternoon. (1)

0.30   Raiding party enter CANADIAN DUGOUTS.

0.30   38th Divisional Artillery will form pockets round points where wire has been cut. Heavy Artillery continue on original targets.

0.40.   Right Group form barrage on German front line and on sap heads behind CANADIAN DUGOUTS from C.22.a.3.2. to Sap 8. (2)

0.60.   Raiders return

1.15   Bombardment gradually dies down.

2.30   )
3.15   )   5 minutes burst of shrapnel on points
4.15   )   where wire has been cut. (3)
5.0 (if foggy morning))

(1) Ammunition allotment as follows:-

    Right Group   18 prs. - 700   B/121 175 rds.
                4.5" Hows - 200

    Left Group   18 prs. - 800   B/121 200 rds.
                4.5" Hows.- 200

    <u>Corps H.A.</u>

    4 - 9.2" Hows. - 40
    3 - 6" Hows.   - 60
    2 - 60 prs.   - 40
    7 - 4.7" guns   - 100.

(2) Details to be arranged between Group and Infantry Brigade Commanders. Ammunition as required. This should not be a heavy barrage unless asked for. The barrage to stop when raiding party are home.

(3) Group Commanders will be responsible for the gaps cut by their Group. Batteries

----

R.A. 38th Divl No. G.S. 866.

S E C R E T

O.C. LEFT GROUP R.F.A.

In continuation of G.S. 856 and 863.
Zero hour tonight will be 11 p.m. Watches will be synchronised by telephone this evening.

(SD) C. GODDARD, Captain R.A.
Brigade Major, 38th D.A.

15.9.1916

2.

OS.C.Batteries,
Left Group R.F.A.

Forwarded for information. ACKNOWLEDGE

15.9.1916

Lieut., R.F.A.
Adjutant Left Group R.F.A.

O.C. Batteries,
    Left Group R.F.A.

    Reference programme for "Z" night, the bombardment will cease at zero. 60, and no more firing will be done until 2.30, when the 5 mins. bursts of shrapnel will take place, as laid down.

Left Group H.Q,
15th Septr.1916

                      Lieut., R.F.A.
                Adjutant Left Group R.F.A.

Army Form C. 2118.

WAR DIARY
or
INTELLIGENCE SUMMARY

121 Bde. R.F.A. VOL 9
September 1916.

(Erase heading not required.)

Place	Date	Hour	Summary of Events and Information	Remarks and references to Appendices
PROVEN.	Sept. 1916. 1-22		From Sept. 1st - Sept. 22nd, 121 Bde. Headquarters were in rest at PROVEN. Battery wagon lines were visited, and came supplied.	
	22nd		On Sept. 22nd, 121 Bde. H.Q. took over the Left Group left Division's command 113th Infantry Brigade; Headquarters at CHATEAU DES TROIS TOURS, BRIELEN; Lt.Col: H.G. Pringle relieving Lieut. P.J. Pobjoy. Batteries included in the Group were - A "B" "D"/121st Bde. and A "B" "D" 119 Bde.	
BRIELEN.			Co-ordinates of Battery positions as follows — A/119 — B 22 d 1.8 B/119 — B 28 c 8.8 and one extract section at C 26 c 34. D/119 — B 22 d 1.8 and B 23 c 5.3. A/121 — B 21 b 5.6 B/121 — B 15 b 5.8 and one section at B 15 a 1.2 D/121 — I 20 c 6.5. (Anti-Aircraft only at present).	
			Generally, the front has been quiet during this period.	

WAR DIARY
or
INTELLIGENCE SUMMARY

Army Form C. 2118.

Place	Date 1916	Hour	Summary of Events and Information	Remarks and references to Appendices
BRIELEN.	Sept. 22-30.		Work has been going on steadily on gun positions & O.P.S, and much revetting & camouflage work has been carried out.	
	28th.		On the night of 28th Sept. a raid was carried out on the KRUPP SALIENT by the 13th Batt. R.W.F. supported by the Artillery of the Left Group, and by the 24th H.A.G. Left Group Operation Orders is attached.	Operation Orders attached.
			Front covered by the Group – C.70.0.9 to C.14.6.5.2	

[signature]
Lt.Col: Cmdg 72 Bde
R.F.A.

SECRET.

A raid will take place on the Enemy's trenches on the night of   through the gap existing at C.14.a.3.2.

ARTILLERY ACTION WILL BE as follows :-

Zero - 0.02.
0.04 - 0.06.

"A"/119 (4 guns) Front line C.14.a.6.1½ - C.14.a.3¾.2½.

"E"/119. (4 guns)   ,,   ,,   C.14.a.3¾.2½ - C.14.a.3½.4.

"B"/119. Enfilade
         Section   Second line C.14.a.6.2½ - C.14.a.5.3½.

"E"/121. 1 Section ,,   ,,   C.14.a.5.3½ - C.14.a.4.5½.

"D"/119. 1 Section Front Line C.14.a.7¾.0.
         1 How.   Second Line C.14.a.4.5½.
         1 How.   Front Line C.14.a.2.6.

"D"/121 1 How.   Second line C.14.a.6.2½. — 0.06 left to C14.a 7¼ a ¾
         1 How.   ,,   ,,   C.14.a.4½.6.

RATE OF FIRE
          18 pdrs, 5 rds per gun per minute.
          4.5" How. 3 rds per gun per minute.
1 Medium and 2 Stokes T.M's will co-operate.

PAUSE.
          There will be a pause of two minutes from 0.0.2
          0.04. when the intense bombardment will be renewed
          0.04 - 0.06.

BARRAGE.
          0.06 - 0.26. (Longer if situation requires.)

"A"/119. Enfilade Section - C.14.a.6.1½ - C.14.a.6.2½.

"A"/119. 4 guns.   - C.14.a.6.3 - C.14.a.8.3. (1 round per gun per minute)

"B"/119. 4 guns.   - C.14.a.3½.4 - C.14.a.4.5½.

"B"/119. Enfilade section - C.14.a.6.2½ - C.14.a.5.3½.

"E"/121. 1 section.   - C.14.a.5.3½ - C.14.a.4.5½.

Howitzers as above

RATE OF FIRE.
          18 pdrs, 3 rds per gun per minute.
          4.5"   1 rd per gun per minute.

(2) continued.

Lieut. INGLETON will act as LAISON Officer and be at point of departure of raiding party with 2 Telephonists. He will be responsible that Visual Communication is maintained between himself and "B"/119. O.P.

Time, temperature and barometer reading will be sent out at 8 p.m.

WAR DIARY.
Sept. 1916.

1st Fired 7 Rds.   B.S.M. Sims reduced to rank of Sergeant

2nd " 37 "   (Registration &c.) Gun line inspected by G.O.C. Division.

3rd " 12 "   Registration

4th " 9 "   " "

5th " 20 "   " " & retaliation.

6th " 7 "   " " Lt. Davies went to Hospital. 14 men confirmed.

7th " 34 "   Registration. Also fired on strong hostile patrol, which was dispersed

8th " 79 "   Heavy retaliation for T.M. bombardment.

9th " 41 "   Registration, also upon hostile working party.
Two guns moved to wire cutting position.

10th " 24 "   Registration.

11th " 31 "   on a Dump with Success

12th " 2 "

13th " 9 "   2Lt. Turner attached to Bty.

14th " 300 "   "Y" Day. Bombarded enemy's front line system.

15th " 900 "   "Z" Day. Cut wire in morning. Bombarded front line in afternoon & supported raid at night. Raid was not successful.

16th   Fired on 3 working parties.

17th Fired 100 Rounds. Wire cutting test at 3500". Three yard gap cut. Wire cutting section brought back.

18th " 100 " Wire cutting (diversion.) Heavy rain all day.

19th " 335 " In support of raid, which was not successful.

20th " 50 " Registration by aeroplane & retaliation.

21st " 13 " On working party & suspected O.P.

22nd " 23 " Registration &c.
23rd " 12 "
24th " 13 "
25   " 12 " } Registration &
26   " 2   " } on small working
27   " 17 " } parties &c.
28   " 17 "
29   " 18 "
30. " 6   "

Ypnard
Capt
Comdg M/a 1 R.F.A.

30-9-16.

War Diary (contd.)

Night 19/20th Sept.

Battery carried out a demonstration in support of a raid on hostile trenches further S.

See operation orders attached.

J.R. Cranston
Col.

B/121

War Diary. Sept 1916.

Normal trench warfare 1st – 9th. Both sides fairly quiet. Battery beyond registration, shot very little.

9th Operation orders for a wire-cutting scheme and bombardment received. Night 9/10th one gun moved forward to position on BOESINGHE – YPRES railway. Range to front line 2200".

Bombardment was reduced from 3 days to 2.

1st day 14th. Bombardment as for Y day (afternoon) 300 rds front line.
2nd day 15th – Z day.
Cut wire with forward gun (175 rds) in morning.
Concentrated bombardment with 4 guns 3 – 5 p.m. 750 rds front and support line. Much damage.
Retaliation slight.
Night firing 258 rds in bursts at various times, covering a raid further S.
See operation orders attached.

SECRET.

LEFT GROUP R.F.A., 36th D.A.

Reference G.S.No. 938, Wire-Cutting and Bombardment will be carried out as under :-

"X" DAY.

As already arranged.

"Y" DAY.

Morning same as "X" day; afternoon :-

B-121	C.13.b.8.8. to C.14.a.1.7.	) Initial bom-
A-121	C.14.a.1.7. to C.14.a.3.4.	) bardment on
B-119	C.14.a.3.4. to C.14.a.6.1½.	) Front Line and
A-119	C.14.a.6.1½ to C.14.c.75.95	) Support Trench-
D-119 (How.)	C.13.b.8.8. to C.14.c.75.95	) es.

"Z" DAY.

Morning completion of wire-cutting by 18 pdrs., where necessary, same as "X" Day.
Afternoon Heavy Bombardment; same objectives as "Y" day. - 18 pdrs. and 4.5" Hows.

"Z" NIGHT

As per programme already issued.

Ammunition allotment for the various bombardments :-
Each 18 pdr. Battery one quarter of total allotment.

The value of zero time for "X", "Y" and "Z" days will be notified as soon as received.

H.Qrs.
9.9.1916

W.H.Cook Lieut., R.F.A.
Adjutant Left Group R.F.A.

S E C R E T.   R.A. 38th Division No.G.S.861.

O.C. LEFT GROUP.

Tomorrow will be "Z" day.

Reference programme for "Z" Day. As much wire-cutting as possible is to be done tomorrow morning.

The ammunition allotment for "X" and "Y" days is not to be exceeded.

The programme for "Z" day is being altered, and will be forwarded as early as possible.

Hours of commencing afternoon bombardment will be notified as soon as possible.

(SD) C. GELDARD,
Captain R.A.
14.9.1918   Brigade Major, 38th D.A.

OS.C.Batteries,
Left Group R.F.A.

Forwarded. Batteries will proceed with wire-cutting tomorrow morning as early as the light will permit. The importance of effectively and expeditiously dealing with the wire-cutting programme cannot be too strongly impressed upon Battery Commanders.

14th September 1918   Lieut., R.F.A.
Adjutant Left Group R.F.A.

S E C R E T.   Copy No..........

OPERATION ORDER NO. 1, BY LIEUT., COL., P.J.PATERSON D.S.O.,
R.F.A., COMMANDING 119th BRIGADE R.F.A., 38th DIVISIONAL ARTY.

Headquarters   Monday   18th Septr. 1916.

(1) INFORMATION.
A raid is to take place on the enemy's trenches on the night of the 19th/20th inst., through a gap to be cut in the wire at C.14.a.3½.2.

(2) INTENTION:-

"A"-119   18 pdrs. }
"B"-119   ::   }
"A"-121   ::   } Will support the raid.
"D"-119   4.5" Hows.}
(2 guns"D"121 ::   }

"B"-121   18 pdrs. }
(1 gun"D"-121 4.5" Hows.) Will create a diversion.

Trench-Mortars will co-operate.

(3) 2/Lieut. M.P.Fitzgerald will act as Liaison Officer accompanying the Raiding Officer, and taking with him two signallers. He will be responsible that visual and telephonic communication is maintained between himself and the O.P. of B-119

(4) WIRE-CUTTING.
A gap at least 40 yards wide will be cut by "A"/119 and "B"/119 as already arranged.

(5) On the night of 19th/20th, at zero time, the Artillery Bombardment will commence, at which time the raiding party will be at point of departure, in front of our wire at C.25 -

Time O 04 - A-119 will bombard the enemy's front line from C.14.a.3.2½. to C.14.a.5½.2.
Time O 04 - B-119 from C.14.a.3½.3½ to C.14.a.5½.2½.
          and C.14.a.4.3½. to C.14.a.5½.2½.
          A-121 one Sec. on Point C.14.a.2½.4.
                one Sec. C.14.a.0.7½.
          D-119 Hows: two C.14.a.0.7½.
                      one C.14.a.2.6.
                      one C.14.a.4.5½.
          D-121   one C.14.a.6.2½.
                      one C.14.a.7½.0.

Rate of fire : 18 pdrs. 5 rds. per gun per minute; 4.5" Hows. 3 rds. per gun per minute.

Till word has been received from Liaison Officer (probably 20 minutes) Batteries will form a pocket as under :-

A-119   - From C.14.a.6.2½ to C.14.a.4.4.
B-119 (2 guns) C.14.a.5½.2. to C.14.a.6.2½.
              C.14.a.4.5½
              C.14.a.4½.4.
A-121   C.14.a.2½.4. to C.14.a.3½.5½.

Howitzers continue on same targets as before.
Rate of fire - 18 pdrs: 3 rounds per gun per minute.
              Howitzers: 1 round per gun per minute.

-2-

OPERATION ORDER NO. 1 (CONTINUED).

A demonstration will take place as follows :-

O. 4. B-121 - 6 guns C.7.c.6.7. to KEEL COT
      D-121 - FORTIN 17.

Rate of fire for first 4 minutes :-
    18 pdrs. - 5 rounds per gun per minute. XF 5 Sec
    4.5" Hows. 3 rounds per gun per minute.
Afterwards reduced to -
    18 pdrs. 2 rounds per gun per minute XF 15 Sec
    4.5" Hows. 1 round per gun per minute.

Zero time will be notified later.

Headquarters   Lieut., Col., R. F. A.
Left Group
18.9.1916   Commanding Left Group . F. A.

Copy No. 1 filed.
         2 R.A. 28th Div.
         3 113th Infantry Brigade.
         4 A - 119
         5 B - 119
         6 D - 119
         7 A - 121
         8 B - 121
         9 D - 121
        10 O.C.Raid.
        11 2/Lt. M. Fitzgerald.
        12 War Diary.
        13

OS.C.Batteries,
    Left Group R.F.A.

        Reference Operation Order No. 1 of yesterday's
date.   Zero time will be 2 a.m. 20th inst.

Headquarters   Lieut., R.F.A.
Left Group R.F.A.   Adjutant Left Group R.F.A.
19.9.1916

WAR DIARY
or
INTELLIGENCE SUMMARY
(Erase heading not required.)

Army Form C. 2118

Place: September

Date	Hour	Summary of Events and Information	Remarks and references to Appendices
1st		In action N of line outskirts of YPRES.	154
5th		2Lt R.H. DEWHIRST joined.	M
9th		Raid on CANADIAN DUG OUTS by 11th S.W.B. Failure.	154
16th-26th		2Lt R.H. DEWHIRST proceeded on Trench Mortar course.	D
18th-28th		2Lt THOMPSON went on leave.	D
28th		2Lt NOBLE went on leave.	D
29th		Raid on CANADIAN DUG OUTS repeated. No success.	157
30th		Patrol of 17th R.W.F. entered CANADIAN DUG OUTS without difficulty, and found nothing there.	R
		The battery had no particular tasks, except the covered trench warfare, and supporting the 2 raids.	20
17th		5 forts and 1 telephone dug-out completely dug out + rebuilt. R. Bs WESTON and Gr. TOWNLEY were awarded the Military Cross. Capt STEPHENSON awarded Military Cross.	

O'Brian —
Captain D.C. Stephenson
Lieut. W.A.C. Stone
Lieut. J. THOMPSON.

2Lt J.H. RIMMER
" M.A. NOBLE
" R.H. DENHIRST (att.)
D. Stephenson Capt

Army Form C. 2118

WAR DIARY
or
INTELLIGENCE SUMMARY

(Erase heading not required.)

D/112

Instructions regarding War Diaries and Intelligence Summaries are contained in F. S. Regs., Part II and the Staff Manual respectively. Title Pages will be prepared in manuscript.

Place	Date	Hour	Summary of Events and Information	Remarks and references to Appendices
LA BRIQUE Left Sec. in action at I.2.a.8.5.	1.		Fired 10 rounds registration. Quiet day. Slight shelling of front trenches with 77mm in C.14.c	
	2.		Registered "S.O.S." lines. Quiet day. (32rnds)	
O.P. FRASCATI (C.14.c.1.6.)	3.		Retaliated on PILCKEM MILL and support trenches for Rifle fire on C.14.C. 9 rounds	Maj. C.F. COOPER to hospital (sick) sick at BOULOGNE
Magazine Man HAMHOEK	4.		Very quiet.	
YPRES	5.		Handed over Left Section guns to D/112 in same position. Took over 4 guns in action at C.1.d.5.a. from 4th D.A. Attached to Left group 4th D.A. (14th Bde. R.F.A.) Zone whole of 29th Div front. [HOOGE to HAMPSHIRE FARM (C.22.a.3.7.)]. Subterranean gun position with covered C.Ts to pits & telephone room. Many O.Ps.	
	6.		No firing. Enemy shelled YPRES in morning with field guns & medium trench guns : about 60 rounds.	
	7.		Re-registered Zero line. Rafale at I.1.8.1.0. and SEXTON HOUSE (J.1.c.1.1.2.). Enemy shelled front line at I5 a & G and St JEAN - 50 rounds.	
	8.		Re-registered trenches in C.29 a. + G. Premature at No 4 gun. 3 of detachment wounded. 28 rounds. No Rifle fire.	360/816 Sgt. JOHN L.W. W/8519 (H. FOWLER W.S. W/3437 T. WATKINS B. wounded by premature
	9.		Re-registered I.6.6. + I.6 G.+d. Also C.30d. 36 rounds. Enemy shelled I.10 c.d. with field guns.	
	10.		Did not fire. Enemy shelled I.4.a.6.3. with 15cm how.	
	11.		Shelled SEXTON HOUSE, OSCAR FARM (I.6.c.0.9½), suspected O.Ps. Also trench at I.6 c.2.5. + I.6 a.3.4. Enemy fired on YPRES & D/121 Bty. position with 15cms. C.T. hit but little damage some I.3.a. + I.1.a shelled in evening.	
	12.		Re-registration of trench I.1.2.a.0.7., Rasse J.1.a.1.4.8! and trench I.6.c.2.5. Slight shelling of I.2.c. and I.1.8. with 77mm + 15mm respectively.	Capt. J.F. BLIGH posted from AH.Q.

1875 Wt. W 593/826 1,000,000 4/15 J.B.C. & A. A.D.S.S./Forms/C.2118.

Army Form C. 2118

WAR DIARY
or
INTELLIGENCE SUMMARY
(Erase heading not required.)

Instructions regarding War Diaries and Intelligence Summaries are contained in F.S. Regs., Part II and the Staff Manual respectively. Title Pages will be prepared in manuscript.

Place	Date	Hour	Summary of Events and Information	Remarks and references to Appendices
YPRES.	13.		Re-registered CKPEL, UHLAN FARM (C.29.B.5.5) and O.Ps on ridge C.30.d.5.9. No enemy activity	
	14.		Did not fire. Very quiet day. Windy.	
	15.	2.50 A.M.	Registered points on ROULERS-OSTEND (ROULERS-COURTRAI) railway for raid.	45109 G. HERBERT Rd.
		11 p.m to 12.15	Bombardment for raid at RAILWAY WOOD. Fired about 400 rounds. Premature at No. 4 gun. 2nd Lt JONES & 2 wounded. Right escaped unhurt. No retaliation	769 Sgt. DANCE H.S. 72490 G. GEE S. 7220 G. DAVID J wounded by premature.
			1 killed, 3 wounded. 2nd Lt Jones the wounds. Relieved by 8/14 29th R.A. R.F.A. detachment returned to LA BRIQUE and took over.	
	16.		Did not fire. Quiet day.	
			Did not fire from D/114	
LA BRIQUE	17.		Did not fire. Quiet day.	
	18.		Did not fire. Quiet day. Very wet. E gun fought into action in turned down pit at ELVERDINGE (2nd Lt M. JONES)	
	19.		Re-registered C.14.a.4.0 and a.6.3.1 for C gun reported as FORTIN 17. raid. Retaliation. All quiet 2.30 a.m.	
	20.	2 a.m	Bombardment for raid. Raid failed. No retaliation.	
			Showery day	
	21.		Did not fire. Some 77mm shell fell in C.20.E. and C.13.E.	
	22.		Enemy a/c shelled PERISCOPE HSE. (C.26.9.9) suspected O.P. 1 direct hit demolishing top half. Registered Fort HENRI C.14.a.17.	
			TURCO FARM shelled by 77mm	

30.9.16.

J.P.R.R.A.
and D/121 Bde R.F.A.

Army Form C. 2118.

Vol/10

WAR DIARY or INTELLIGENCE SUMMARY

121st &131st R.F.A. Left Group R.F.A.
October 1916

(Erase heading not required.)

Place	Date	Hour	Summary of Events and Information	Remarks and references to Appendices
BRIELEN	October 1916		Artillery - 4 Batteries - CHATEAU DES TROIS TOURS - Left Group R.F.A. Batteries under captain Lipscombe (recently rejoined D/121 after having been moved on report of - 30th - 31st Oct) to use brigade in 7.C.8.2.	
	14th	2.30 pm	Bombardment of front line at C.19.a.4.2 by 9.2 Hows. in preparation for raid by 13th R.I.F. About 60 rounds were fired, doing damage. In consequence of German harassing fire activities against our trenches a scheme was prepared for counter-battery retaliation by all batteries in Canal Trenches cliffs in Siegfried. The scheme is otherwise 1770 to be used on demand.	"MINNIE"
			Another scheme was prepared atmosphere against 4 Division for retaliation by short bursts of bombardment on O.P. front in conjunction with Right Group R.F.A. See "Minnies Scheme" This scheme has been used Guns are less by day on "MINNIE" lines	"SPLASH."
	12th		On the night Oct 12 O'clock an raid (on had by the 13th R.I.F. (119 Infantry Bde.) on the Junction North at C.19.a.4.2. Quaker Oats is attacked. The raid was successful, 1 prisoner captured, the action suffered from our 18 pdr. but the infantry 9.2 Hows. cooperated letter from OC.13th R.I.F. to OC Left Group R.F.A. attached	"RAJA"
	13th		On 13th Oct. wire cutting took place at C.19.a 0.7 in preparation for raid by 19th R.I.F. This was carried out by 18 pdr enfilade section. The Heavy Artillery cooperated C.7.0.6.7 with 9.2 Hows. Simultaneously	

Army Form C. 2118.

WAR DIARY or INTELLIGENCE SUMMARY

(Erase heading not required.)

12, Bde. R.F.A. Oct. 1916.

Place	Date	Hour	Summary of Events and Information	Remarks and references to Appendices
BRIELEN.	Oct 1916 13th		On the night of Oct. 13 a raid was carried out by the enemy trenches at C.13.b.9½.7¾. It was preceded by a 15 minute bombardment by Stokes mortars, and also by a box barrage of H.C.)C.67 & mortars the enemy's. This raid (about 20 "success"). A machine gun + prisoner were captured and identification obtained. The trenches were found to be badly damaged by artillery & Stokes fire, + the German infantry suffered considerable casualties. Heavy Artillery (again cooperated with 9.2 How.s, as did also the Belgian Artillery (5th D.A.) The Infantry again proposed themselves very pleased with the Artillery arrangements; a copy of letter from G.O.C. 113th Inf. Bde. is attached.	"Raid B." Letter.
	26th		A quiet 10 days followed then this raid: Scheme was prepared for Rhine raid, and S.O.S. barrage revised. Arrangement to cooperate with the Belgians on our North was also recommitted in conjunction with the Command of the 5th D.A. (Belgian). A french mortar shoot took place on 25th at C.7.C.67 in preparation for raid in this sector. The shoot was covered by left group batteries, a	Op. Order No. 8.

Army Form C. 2118.

WAR DIARY
or
INTELLIGENCE SUMMARY
(Erase heading not required.)

121st Bde. R.F.A. Oct. 1916

Place	Date	Hour	Summary of Events and Information	Remarks and references to Appendices
BRIELEN	October 1916			
	28th	11am-3pm	Two shoots B/A. fired on D38 and on C7c67 in further preparation for the Raid and on C14 a 3,3,4, to widen the breach in the German parapet & thicken the enemy's attention. See attached Operation Order.	Operation Order No. 6 A
		3 pm	From 3.0 to 3.25 pm a Trench Mortar shoot was carried out on C7c67 to further widen gap in enemy wire. Covered by Artillery fire from all Bdes of 121 RFA as per attached Order. The shoot was found by the raiders to have been successful in cutting the wire, although the latter was very difficult to see.	Operation Order No. 8
	29th	3pm	A short intense bombardment was carried out by B/121 and D/121 (How.) from 3.0 pm to 6.0. C14 a 1/2 6 1/2 Object - to distract attention from C7c67. B/121 fired 100 rounds, D/121 50. The shoot was very good results, the parapet badly knocked.	
	29th	11.30 pm	The Raid on C7c67 was carried out by 16th R.W.F. It attacked enemy trenches. The Raid was a great success (Major G.O. Parker part.) It was successful. Sane (Major Farmer Rifles) and few casualties sustained. In spite of kit mud, careful registration was done & fastened arrangements were perfect. Result. Later. A prisoner 7 Suffolk Reserve Regiment captured by Belgians stated that the casualties from our bombardment were 200 killed & wounded.	Operation Order No 7

Army Form C. 2118.

WAR DIARY
or
INTELLIGENCE SUMMARY
(Erase heading not required.)

121. Bde. R.F.A. Oct 1916.

Place	Date	Hour	Summary of Events and Information	Remarks and references to Appendices

BRIELEN	October 18		Attached is a scheme for Co-operation with the Belgians in case of hurried wasps for activity on the Army front. Throughout the month the activity of the enemy's artillery has been very little, and even retaliation during Raids is as a rule feeble.
			
			Batteries in the Group:—
			A/121
			B/121
			D/121
			    A/119
			    B/119
			    D/119	

	24th.		On 24th Oct. B/121 less 2 howitzers to D/119.	
	31st.		D/121, whose 2 howitzers were rushed into action their 2 hours. Its new position at 12cD.2, in YPRES. The new position is still in course of construction. Work has been going on continuously on gun positions, O.P.s, wagon lines	

H.M. Pringle
Lieut. Colonel, R.F.A.
Commanding:-
121st Brigade, R.F.A.

SECRET.

A Bombardment of the Front Line by 9.2" Hows. will take place this afternoon (10th instr) from 2.30. onwards.

Batteries will stand by to reply to reply to any German retaliation, their guns laid on the same targets as ordered for sections in order for "MINNIE" retaliation.

Powell M.
for
Lieut. Colonel R.F.A.
10-10-16. Commanding LEFT GROUP R.F.A.

MINNIE.

SECRET.

In order to check the present activity of the German Trench Mortar, the following action will be carried out by the Artillery of the LEFT GROUP.

Batteries will keep guns loaded and laid as under :-

A/119. 1 Section Search from C.14.a.9.0. - C.14.b.2.1.
B/119. 1 Section Trench Junction about   C.14.a.2.6.
  ,,   Enfilade Section Search C.14.a.1.9½ - C.8.c.2.1.
A/121. 1 Section Sweep.   C.8.c.2.2½ - C.8.c.1.6.
B/121. 1 Section Search   C.7.d.7.8½ - C.8.c.0.9.
D/121. Triangle of trenches & Tramways about C.14.a.3.5.
D/119. 1 Section. Triangle of trenches & Tramway about C.14.a.5½.9.
  ,,   1 Section Trench Junction about C.8.c.2.2½.

When the Infantry Brigade inform Group Headquarters that Retaliation for "MINNIE" is required, the word "MINNIE" will be sent to each Battery.   On receipt of this order the 18 pdr. sections above mentioned will at once fire 2 rounds gunfire followed by 3 rounds a gun at 5 seconds intervals, the first 2 rounds being Shrapnel and the remainder H.E.

The 4.5" Hows. will fire 4 rounds a gun, deliberate Detachments will then stand by to repeat, until orders are received from Group Headquarters to "Stand easy".

If "MINNIE" is sent by night, guns will be got on to these targets as rapidly as possible and the same procedure followed.

This cancels all previous orders.

H. Pringle
Lieut-Colonel R.F.A.
Commanding LEFT GROUP R.F.A.

9-10-16.

SPLOSH.

O.C.   A/119th Brigade R.F.A.

A system is being arranged for mutual co-operation between Groups, to deal with hostile activity by means of an intense concentrated retaliation.

The signal for this joint retaliation will be the word "SPLOSH" sent over the telephone, followed by the time at which the retaliation is to take place.

Thus, if at 12.15 p.m. the words "SPLOSH" 12.40 p.m." are sent, all guns which can fire on the objectives ordered will open 3 rounds gun fire at 12.40 p.m.

It is recognised that in some cases this fire will be unobserved and unregistered.

Until further notice, the special objective for this "SPLOSH" retaliation will be the Trench Junctions at about C.14.b.6.6.

Please let me know at once whether any of your guns can NOT fire on this objective.

Lieut-Colonel R.F.A.

12-10-16.   Commanding LEFT GROUP R.F.A.

Reference ST. JULIEN Trench Map.
Scale 1/10,000, Edition 3D.

SECRET.   Raid A

A raid will take place on the Enemy's trenches on the night of 12/13 Oct through the gap existing at C.14.a.4½.2. The raiding party will leave by that gap and by another about C.14.a.3¾.3

ARTILLERY ACTION WILL BE AS FOLLOWS :-

Zero - 0.03.

"A"/119. (4 guns) Front Line C.14.a.6½.1. - C.14.a.5.2.

"B"/119. (4 guns) ,, ,, C.14.a.5.2. - C.14.a.3½.4.

"B"/119. Enfilade Section. Second Line
C.14.a.6.2½. - C.14.a.5.3½.

"B"/121. 1 Section Second Line C.14.a.5.3½. - C.14.a.4.5½.

"D"/119. 1 Section Front Line C.14.a.7¾.0.
1 How. Second Line. C.14.a.4.5½.
1 How. Front Line. C.14.a.2.6.

"D"/121. 1 How. Second Line. C.14.a.6.2½.
1 How. ,, ,, C.14.a.4½.6.

RATE OF FIRE.
18 pdrs, 5 rds per gun per minute.
4.5" Hows. 3 rds per gun per minute.
1 Medium and the Stokes Trench Mortars' will co-operate.
During the 9.2" How. Bombardment from 3 p.m. - 5.30 p.m. 3rd inst, 1 Medium and 1 Stokes Trench Mortar will cut wire opposite C.14.a.3¾.3.

BARRAGE.
0.03 - 0.33. (Longer if situation requires)

"A"/119. Enfilade Section - C.14.a.6.1½. - C.14.a.6.2½.

"A"/119. 1 Section - C.14.a.6½.3. - C.14.a.8.3. (1 rd per gun per minute)

"B"/119. (4 guns) - C.14.a.3½.4. - C.14.a.4.5½. (2 rds per gun per minute)

"B"/119. Enfilade Section - C.14.a.6.2½. - C.14.a.5.3½.

"B"/121. 1 Section. - C.14.a.5.3½. - C.14.a.4.5½.

Howitzers as above, except 1 How. "D"/121., firing on C.14.a.6.2½, which will lift to C.14.a.7½.4½.

RATE OF FIRE.
18 pdrs, 3 rds per gun per minute.
4.5" Hows. 1 rd per gun per minute.

S E C R E T.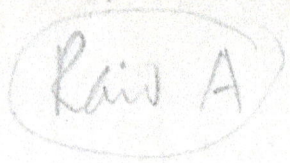

      Following Amendments to Orders for RAID will take place during the "Barrage" from 0.03 - 0.33 (or longer)

Section "A"/119. from C.14.a.6½.3. - C.14.a.8.3. is cancelled.
"B"/119. from C.14.a.3½.4. - C.14.a.4.5¼. for 4 Guns red 1 Section.

Right Group will provide 3 - 4.5" Hows. to engage following points :

        1 How. - ESSEN ~~KILN~~ FARM
        ~~1 How.~~ - ~~C.14.a.3.4.~~
        1 How. - C.14.a.3½.4½.

                Lieut. Colonel R.F.A.

                Commanding LEFT GROUP R.F.A.

S E C R E T.

   Following Amendments to Orders for RAID will take place during the "Barrage" from 0.03 - 0.33 (or longer)

Section "A"/119. from C.14.a.6½.3. - C.14.a.8.3. is cancelled.
"B"/119. from C.14.a.3½.4. - C.14.a.4.5¼. for 4 Guns red 1 Section.

Right Group will provide 3 - 4.5" Hows. to engage following points :

    1 How. - ESSEN ~~KOLN~~ FARM
    ~~1 How.~~ - ~~C.14.a.3.4.~~
    1 How. - C.14.a.3½.4½.

          Lieut. Colonel R.F.A.

         Commanding LEFT GROUP R.F.A.

O.C. Batteries Left Group Brigade R.F.A.

The following letter has been received:-
"O.C. LEFT GROUP R.F.A.

May I on behalf of the 13th Batt. R.W.Fus. thank you and all Officers and men under your Command for all the trouble taken for us in our last two raids.

All ranks speak in unstinted praise of both BARRAGES put up and I think that the confidence which the men of this Battalion have now got in Artillery fire will have a much more far reaching result than any success we may have obtained.

Will you convey to all ranks and let them know that we consider that any success we may have obtained is owing to the Artillery work and as we want the R.F.A. to share all honours with us
(sd) R.C.CAMPBELL Lt.Col.
Commanding 13th Batt. R.W.Fus."

The Group Commander congratulates all ranks on this second success.

2/Lt. R.F.A.
Adjutant LEFT GROUP R.F.A.

12-10-16.

A D C01.

Brigade Major,
R.A., 38th Division.

Wire cutting C.14.a.0.7½ will take place about 10 a.m. on the 13th.

C.27 & E.28 should be cleared by 10 a.m. till 11.30 a.m. Simultaneously the H.A. will bombard C.7.c.6.7. with either 12" or 9.2" Hows.

ESSEX TRENCH should be cleared (C.7.c.6½.1.. to Junction with FARGATE.)

An Officer from the 15th. R.W.F. Raiding Party should be at the Contour 19 C.I. Off HUDDERSFIELD ROAD by 9.45 a.m. on the 13th inst.

Lieut.Colonel R.F.A.

12-10-16.   Commanding LEFT GROUP R.F.A.

Raid "B" Amendments.

Bombardment.

Cancel B/121's action and insert

"B" 119 Enfilade section − C.14.a. 1/2.5 3/4 − C.14 a 1/2.7 3/4
"B" 121 4 guns   − C.14.a 1/2.7 1/4 − C.13 b. 8 1/2. 8

Order for Hows.

"D" 119 1 How French Junction C.8.c.1.1/2
         1 How   "   "   C.8 c 1 3/4. 2 1/2
         1 How (forward section) C.14.a. 2 1/2. 8
         1 How   "   "   C.14.a. 3. 8 1/4

H.M.Pringle
Lt.Col. cmdg.
Left Group. R.F.A.

Raid B.

S/C T.

A RAID will take place at C.13.b.5½.7½ on the night of the 13th/14th Oct.

The RAID will be preceded by a bombardment by Trench Mortars from Zero − 0.18 minutes.

ARTILLERY ACTION WILL BE AS FOLLOWS :−

0.14 − 0.18 Bombardment.

1½.5¾

"D"/121.   C.14.a.1.6½ − C.13.b.5¾.8.
"D"/119. 1 Section. SALIENT at C.14.a.31.39.   ← lift to C8c 2.2½ during Barrage
  "   1 How.   TRENCH JUNCTION C.8.c.1.4.
  "   1 How.   "   "   C.8.d.12.2½.
"D"/121. 1 How.   "   "   C.14.b.2½.5.
  "   1 How.   "   "   C.14.a.5.8½.

RATE OF FIRE.
        18 pdrs − 3 rds per gun per minute.
        4.5" How. − 2 rds per gun per minute.

BARRAGE
        0.18 − 0.38 (longer if required)

"B"/119. 1 Section Right Flank. C.14.a.1.7. − C.14.a.2½.8.
  "   1 Section Left Flank. C.14.a.8½.8. − C.7.d.9½.1.
  "   1 Sect. (ENFILADE) 2nd LINE C.14.a.2½.7. − C.14.a.1.9½.
"A"/119. ENFILADE SECTION.   C.14.a.1.9½ − C.8.c.1.2.
"B"/121. 1 Section.   C.7.d.9½.5. − C.8.c.1½.1.

Howitzers as above. Except no How. D/119. (see above note).

RATE OF FIRE.
        18 pdrs "B"/119. − 3 rds per gun per minute.
        " Remainder − 2 rds per gun per minute.
        4.5" How.   − 1 rd per gun per minute.

Wire will be cut at point of entry by the Enfilade Section of "B"/119. during the 12th inst.   100 rds may be expected.

Lieut   with two telephonists will be with O.C. RAID in our Front Line trenches and will arrange visual signalling with "B"/119's O.P.

        Watches will be synchronized and Barometer and Thermometer readings will be sent out at times to be arranged later.

AMMUNITION
        Total expenditure :−   18 pdr. − 710 rds.
                               4.5" How. − 156 rds.

"Bombardment" ... all Shrapnel.
Barrage --- Right & Left Flank
            Shrapnel.
       " --- Rest HE.

                                    Pringle
                                    Lieut-Colonel R.F.A.
                                    Commanding

O.C.		Brigade R.F.A.

The Group Commander wishes all ranks to know that this morning he had a message from O.C. RAID 15th R.W.Fus. and afterwards a personal call from the Battalion Commander, to thank the Artillery for their work last night.

Message says:- "All guns landed their shells perfectly."

A further congratulatory letter has been received from Brig-General T.PRICE DAVIES which reads as follows :-
"I have again to write and congratulate you and your Officers on their excellent work in connection with the two raids which have been such a success." All ranks in this Brigade appreciate the thorough and efficient manner in which the Artillery arrangements were carried out.
Our success has been largely due to your efforts."
			(sd) T.PRICE DAVIES. Brig.Gen.
			Commanding 113th Infantry Brigade.

14-10-16.
				Powell 2/Lt.R.F.A.
				Adjutant LEFT GROUP R.F.A.

SECRET.

Operation Order No 6A.

On the 28th October.

A/121.)
B/121. (C.7.c.6.7.
D/121.)

18 pdrs.   150 rds H.E.
4.5" Hows. 100 rds H.E.

A/119.)
B/119. (C.14.a.3½.4.
D/119.)

125 rds each H.E. per 18 pdr.
100 rds   H.E. per 4.5" How.

Both shoots to be deliberate.

In the case of C.14.a.3½.4. the object is to increase the existing gap in the parapet.

In the case of C.7.c.6.7. the object is to

    (1) To breach the parapet.

    (2) to destroy any unseen wire in front of the parapet.

In this shoot the batteries concerned will endeavour to get 20% of their rounds short of the parapet to destroy wire.

The above shoots must take place between 11 a.m. and 3 p.m. tomorrow 28th October.

    A C K N O W L E D G E.

27-10-16.

Lieut. Colonel R.F.A.
Commanding LEFT GROUP R.F.A&

SECRET.

Operation Order No 8.

Covering fire will be required for Trench Mortar Shoot this afternoon between 3 p.m. – 3.25 p.m.

A/121. 1 Section.   C.7.a.3½.1½. – C.7.a.7½.3½.
B/121. Front Line, FARM 14., FORTIN 17.
B/119. Enfilade Section. C.7.a.2½.0. – C.7.a.2.4½.
D/121. 1 Gun.   C.7.a.1.1.
        1 Gun.   B.12.b.9.2.
D/119. 1 Section.   B.12.b.9.8.

RATE OF FIRE.

A/121. & B/119. Section fire 30 seconds.
B/121.   ,,   ,, 40   ,,
   Hows.   1 rd per gun per 2 minutes.

TIME – will be sent out at 2 p.m.

ACKNOWLEDGE.

Lieut. Colonel R.F.A.
Commanding LEFT GROUP R.F.A.

28-10-16.

SECRET.   OPERATION ORDER – NO. 7.

A RAID will be carried out by the 16th R.W.Fus. at C.7.c.6.7. on the night of the 29th/30th.

Medium and STOKES Mortars will bombard this point previous to the RAID.   Wire will be cut by Medium Trench Mortars and Artillery as may be found necessary.

ARTILLERY PROGRAMME will be as follows :-
BOMBARDMENT - Zero 0.03½ B/121. 4 Guns C.7.c.6.7.–C.7.c 7¾.7¾.
              Zero.0.04. B/119. Enfilade
                                  Section.C.7.c.6.7.–C.7.c.5.8.
              Ditto.   D/121. 1 Section. FORTIN 17.
                          D/119. 1 Section. C.7.c.9¾.7¾.
                            1   ,,   C.7.c.1¾.9½.

BARRAGE.–0.03½ – 0.40 (longer if required or till order "stop" is sent
              From 0.04 minutes. B/119. Enfilade
                                  Section C.7.d.1.7.–C.7.c.9.7½.
                          A/119. Enfilade
                                  Section C.7.c.9.7½.–C.7.c.6¼.8.
              (one gun remaining on C.7.d.6¼.8.)
                          A/121. C.7.c.5.8¼.–C.7.a.3.0.
                          B/121. C.7.a.3½.1½.–C.7.a.7¼.½.

Howitzers as above.
RATES OF FIRE –
       BOMBARDMENT:– 18 pdrs. 5 rds per gun per minute.
                    4.5" Hows. 3 rds per gun per minute.
       BARRAGE:–   18 pdrs. 3 rds per gun per minute. (except B/121
                    who will fire at 1 rd per gun per minute.)
                    4.5" Hows. 1 rd per gun per minute.
                                               0.24–0.40 2 rds per gun per minute.
EXTRA BARRAGE.

10 minutes after the order "STOP" is received the 18 pdr Batteries forming the "BARRAGE" except B/121. will re-open on the same lines as the Barrage at 5 rds per gun per minute for 2 minutes. B/121. and all Hows. will turn on C.7.c.6.7. also for 2 minutes.
                    18 pdrs. at 5 rds per gun per minute.
                    4.5" Hows.   3 rds per gun per minute.

:-2- Continued.

BELGIAN Trench Mortars will be invited to co-operate.
Lieut.   with two operators will be at the point
of our Front Line where the RAIDERS leave and will be responsible
that telephone and Visual signalling is established with B/121's
O.P.

A C K N O W L E D G E.

Lieut. Colonel R.F.A.
26-10-16.   Commanding LEFT GROUP R.F.A.

Copy. No. 1.   A/121.
     2.   B/121.
     3.   D/121.
     4.   A/119
     5.   B/119
     6.   D/119.

S E C R E T.

In the event of "BELGIAN MINNIE" being sent out Howitzers of the LEFT GROUP will engage targets as under :-

D/121. 1 Gun CARREE FARM (B.6.a.1.7½.)

1 Gun N.E. Corner of BOIS des CRAPOUILLOTS's (B.6.d.0.7¾.)

D/119. 1 Section. Trench Mortars at B.6.d.3.2. just South of STEAM MILL.

1 Section. Trench Mortars at B.12.b.7¾.7¼.

5 rounds per gun will be fired. These points should be registered as soon as possible. (D/121. after getting into new position.)

M. BRACQ, LIAISON Officer will conduct Officers to Belgian O.P's whence the targets can be seen.

Lieut. Colonel R.F.A.
Commanding LEFT GROUP R.F.A.

31-10-16.

WAR DIARY
INTELLIGENCE SUMMARY

Army Form C. 2118

October 1916

C/121

Place	Date	Hour	Summary of Events and Information	Remarks and references to Appendices
	9		Still in action in Northern outskirts of YPRES.	
			Lieut NOBLE returned from leave.	
	13		Supported raid. Artillery fire accurate. Raid a failure.	
			The Whitewashed - Rubbish heap Crossroads in full swing. Otherwise a very dull month.	
			Officers with battery:-	
			Captain D.T. Skipworth	
			Lieut W.A. C. Stone	
			2nd Lieut J.H. Rimmer	
			" J. Thompson	
			" In a hosp.	
			" R.H. Bestwick (attached)	

D.T. Skipworth
Capt R.F.A.
Comdg C/121

Army Form C. 2118.

WAR DIARY
or
INTELLIGENCE SUMMARY
(Erase heading not required.)

121st. Bde. R.F.A.   November 1916.

Vol XI

Place	Date	Hour	Summary of Events and Information	Remarks and references to Appendices
BRIELEN.	November 1916		From Nov. 1st till Nov. 30th 1916, 121st. Bde. Hd. Qrs. was still at TROIS TOURS CHATEAU in command of Left Group, 30th. Dn. under Lt. Col. H.G. Pringle. RFA. A, B, and D batteries 121 Bde. are in H.Q. Group, in their old positions; C/121 is under the Right Group, in the Glass Houses YPRES. The enemy are still quiet, assertion action always from our side. Special attention has been paid by us to the enemy lines in C.14.a, and the KRUPP salient, where he has recently damaged the enemy trenches, entanglements, consequently much enemy work has gone on, and many working parties have been caught by our fire. 1st month the enemy's Gunners 97th. 113th. Inf. Bde. reported that reactions found of/and are continually heard. Gunfire at and just behind CAESAR'S NOSE, (C.13.b.6.) (C.13.b.i.B.) The resultant was the Regiment (attacked) called 'CAESAR', the code word sent out for that this concerned whenever the infantry have this work going on. Attached to the month has been cooperation with the 4.6.16 Squadron RFC. Much useful registration. Chiefly 84's Horn & has been done by aeroplane, and nearly to have done some counter battery work on hostile battery with near: specially a battery at C.1.d.9.2.3.), which was reported to have been silenced but 9.2.1.3 known, doubtful, as the further was again reported active. Off. Some time of Ginchereum	For detail Diary CAESAR.

WAR DIARY or INTELLIGENCE SUMMARY

Army Form C. 2118.

Brig. W.
Gen. Cmdg.
12/151732 R.F.A.

12/151732 R.F.A.

Nov 1916

Place	Date	Hour	Summary of Events and Information	Remarks and references to Appendices
RIELEN	Nov. 1915		Some evening & hostile batteries are usually seen on 65th Counter-Battery Group, and have proved useful between 4th Div. in occupation has been the wiring-up rails between L/H Group R.G.A. and the Counter Battery Group, and also the 29th Siege Group R.G.A. under Lt. Col. G.N. Baggard. At 1 a.m. on the 14/15 Nov. a Stokes Mortar shoot took place on CAESAR'S NOSE, which was carried by our artillery fire.	
	14th			
	17th		On the 17th Nov. 11 p.m. a concentrated raid was carried out by the Right Brigade on the HIGH COMMAND R REDOUBT. Further support, A/119 and D/12 were four artillery the R. Group Commander with the L/H Group will the remaining Batteries. Carried out a demonstration which Hurdle-fire and attached programme. This was preceded on his way by Contactment C/14 a Sec. by heavy and field guns & howrs, and by immediate two points at C/14 a. Much damage was done. Energy in barrage & punitive trench & dugouts bombed & punitive kicks. Enemy retaliation was slight, and little ammunition.	
	25th		On 25th Nov. at 5 p.m. a salvo was arranged in the trench & train Junction C8c 2.2, Art guns & howitzers in VIII & 15th Corps H.A. and all in L/H Group, firing one round arth burst at 5 min. intervals; 10 F.A. field Service Guns of Shrapnel late in the evening to catch hostile working parties as at the spot.	
	27th		At 7.20 p.m. the guns opened rapidly fire and Thr. This all along our front. No retaliation found and air guns a barrage. The enemy was not silenced till about 8.30 p.m.) but no infantry action took place. Our barrels were reported to have been very effective & well directed.	
	30th		Arrangements have been made the Inhabitants Office worked by our O.P.S. In order attached. Newton bombs constructed by Neuros, Gov. constructed to	

Bart. C/121 noting 1000 him.
2449 Wt. W14957/Mgo 750,000 1/16 J.B.C. & A. Forms/C.2118/12.

WAR DIARY or INTELLIGENCE SUMMARY

Army Form C. 2118

C/121.

November 1916.

Place	Date	Hour	Summary of Events and Information	Remarks and references to Appendices
	10th		Still in action on northern outskirts of Ypres.	
	16th		Lt DEWHIRST left the battery for Trench Mortars.	
			Supported raid by 14th & Welch on HIGH COMMAND REDOUBT. Great success. Many congratulations on the battery's shooting were received by Lieut STONE, who was commanding during Capt. Stephenson's absence on leave.	
	28th to 29th		Covered Trench Mortar bombardment in connection with raid by 55th Div.	
			Officers present.	
			Capt. D.C. Stephenson	
			Lieut. W.A.C. Stone	
			Lieut. G.H. Rimmer	
			" J. Thompson	
			" M.A.P. Noble	

B.S.M. C.H. Thompson.

D.C. Stephenson Capt
Comdg C/121.

S E C R E T.   "CAESAR"

B/119.	4 guns.	2x12 C.13.b.8.8. — C.7.d.9¾.1.
	Enfilade section.	C.14.a.1.9½. — C.8.c.2.2½.
A/121.	4 guns.	C.14.a.2½.8. — C.14.a.1.9½.
D/119.	1 section.	C.13.b.8.8.
	1 ,,	C.14.a.2½.8. — C.14.a.1.9½.
D/121.	1 ,,	C.14.a.1.9½. — C.8.c.2.2½.

1 Salvo followed by 3 rounds gun fire.

    i.e. 40 rounds - 18 pdr.

          24 ,, 4.5" How.

If work continues order "Repeat".

                                            Lieut. Colonel R.F.A.
                                        Commanding LEFT GROUP R.F.A.

O.C.   A /121st Brigade R.F.A.

Infantry Officers will visit CHEAPSIDE and CANAL BANK O.P. daily henceforth and must be given every assistance to learn the front.

R.A. Officers must also frequently visit first line trenches to study the front from the Infantry point of view. A guide to shew officers the way to CHEAPSIDE will be at MODDER FM. daily at 10 a.m.; and at midday as well, on Mondays, Wednesdays, & Fridays.

Powell M/c Lieut. Colonel R.F.A.
10-11-16.   Commanding LEFT GROUP R.F.A.

SECRET.   OPERATION ORDER No. OX

A 12" Howitzer is registering KULN FARM this afternoon
commencing at 2 p.m.
          After 3rd and 6th rounds Batteries as under will fire
1 Salvo followed by 1 round gun fire :-

B/119.   C.14.a.6.2½. : - C.14.a.8.7½.
A/121.   C.14.b.3.5. : - C.14.b.3.5.
B/121.   C.14.a.8.7½. : - C.14.a.5.9½.
Half Shrapnel and Half H.E.

All Batteries to be prepared to reply to enemy retaliation
If Retaliate "MINNIE" sent :-above batteries and D/119. fire
1 salvo followed by 2 rounds gun fire on C.14.a.5½.9. from all guns.

If Retaliate "ARTILLERY" sent 18 pdr batteries fire 1 salvo
followed by 2 rounds gun fire on Night lines.
B/119. then fire 30 rounds on C.14.a.3½.4.
D/119.   ,, 20 ,,   ,, C.14.a.1.7.

                                   Lieut. Colonel R.F.A.
14-11-16.   Commanding LEFT GROUP R.F.A.

S E C R E T.

A Raid will be carried out on HIGH COMMAND REDOUBT by the 14th (Welsh) Regt. on X day.

LEFT GROUP 38th D.A. (less A/119 & D/121.) will make a demonstration to divert the enemy's attention from the actual point.

The demonstration will be on front line from C.14.a.3½.4. to C.14.a.1.7. and will take place on W & X days.

PROGRAMME as follows :-

W. day.
....
10 a.m. - 1 p.m.
    12" Howitzers fire 40 rounds from C.14.a.3½.4.-C.14.a.1.7.

1 p.m. - 2 p.m.
       D/119.   200 rounds.   C.14.a.3½.4. - C.14.a.1.7.

2 p.m. - 2.30 p.m.
    B/119. Enfilade Section. Cut gap in wire extending
        40 yards N.W. from C.14.a.3½.4.
        (150 rounds) 60% Shrapnel.

2.30 p.m. - 3.30 p.m.
    B/119. 300 rounds H.E.   C.14.a.3½.4. - C.14.a.1.7.

(3)

0.01 – 0.02. BOMBARDMENT.
(1 minute before Zero)

    A/121.   C.14.a.3½.4. – C.14.a.1.6.
    B/119. 4 guns.   ,,   ,,
    D/119. 1 How.   C.14.a.6.2½.
           1 How.   C.8.c.2.2½. –
           1 Section. C.14.a.8.0. – C.14.a.8¾.0.

RATE OF FIRE –
        18 pdr. 6 rounds per gun per minute.
        4.5" How. 3   ,,   ,,   ,,

0.02 – 0.05 LIFT.

A/121.   } C.14.a.4¼.6. – C.14.a.1.9½.
B/119. 4 guns.}
B/121. 4 guns. C.14.a.1.9½. – C.8.c.2.2½.
Hows. as above.

RATE OF FIRE –
        18 pdrs. 4 rds per gun per minute.
        4.5" Hows. 3 ,, ,, ,,

0.05 – 0.35 BARRAGE. *(40)*

A/121. 4 guns. C.14.a.4¼.6. – C.14.a.1.9½.
  1. 60 pdr. Enfilade. ,,   ,,
B/119. 1 Section. C.14.a.9.0. – C.14.b.1½.1. ← *increase to 3 rds per gun per min. at 0.35.*
      1 ,,   C.14.a.1.7. – C.14.a.2½.8.
    Enfilade ,,   C.14.a.3½.4. – C.14.a.4.6.
B/121. 1 Section. C.14.b.0.7. – C.14.a.5½.8.
      1 ,,   C.14.a.5½.9.
      1 ,,   C.14.a.1.9½. – C.8.c.2.2½.

Hows.
D/119. 1 How. ESSEN FARM.
      1 How. KOLN FARM.
      1 Section. C.14.a.8.0. – C.14.a.8¾.0. *increase to 2 rds per gun per minute at 0.35.*

RATE OF FIRE –
      18 pdrs. 0.05 – 0.20. 2 rds per gun per minute.
        ,,   0.20 – 0.35. 1 rd ,, ,,
      4.5" Hows.   1 rd ,, ,,

(4)

0.35 - 0.45.

B/119.   1 Section.   C.14.a.8.0. - C.14.a.8¾.0.
         1   ,,   C.14.a.9.0. - C.14.b.1½.1.
Hows. as in 0.05 - 0.35 Barrage.

RATE OF FIRE.
            18 pdrs.   3 rds per gun per minute.
            4.5" Hows. 2 rds   ,,   ,,

Watches will be synchronized at Right Group Headquarters at
3 p.m. X day.   If possible an Officer should be sent.

                                Lieut. Colonel R.F.A.
                          Commanding LEFT GROUP R.F.A.

WAR DIARY or INTELLIGENCE SUMMARY

Army Form C. 2118.

121st. Bde. RFA.

Place	Date	Hour	Summary of Events and Information	Remarks and references to Appendices
POPERINGHE	Dec. 1916		121st. Bde. H.Q. located at HAMHOEK with Brigade wagon lines. Batteries of 121st. Bde. were still in action during the first half of the month under Col. Paterson, 115th. Bde, Canls Group, with the exception of C/121 whenever heavy Cdr. Rudkin Rifle Group. No rest from fatigues & reliefs during this time. Work and repair of his including construction [?] views rgd of B.T.C. /121, and of the best lines for H.Q. staff & [?] On the nights of 14th-15th and 15th-16th the Divisional artillery was relieved in the line by the 38th. Div. artillery, supported by positions which were taken over with the exception of A/121 Gun position which was vacated by that battery on the night of 15th/16 and left Emp. K. and 67th extension 4ton Butler lui on the left. Wagon lines were taken over on 15th, A/ Bde. H.Q. being relieved by 79th Bde. H.Q. On 15th Dec. the Brigade marched to WATOU, taking over wagon lines from 38th Divl. Artillery. The Brigade was in Corps Reserve.	
WATOU	Dec 14th 16th			
	Dec. 15.		Christmas was spent at WATOU, and celebrated by fluents in full Xmas fare & tactile recuperation.	

Army Form C. 2118.

WAR DIARY
or
INTELLIGENCE SUMMARY
(Erase heading not required.)

Place	Date	Hour	Summary of Events and Information	Remarks and references to Appendices
WATOU. BCOS.			Brigade	
	28.		competition was held on Sept. further weights, and on 25th Christmas dinner, training carried, and a Brigade Officers dinner in the evening. On 28th a concert was given by the Brigade to the Cinema hall.	
	29.		On Dec 29th the Brigade marched out of WATOU & went to training ground at WISSANT near Calais, i.e.	
	30.		one spent at LEDERZEELE, the second at NORDAUSQUES,	
	31.		and the third, 31st, a 20 mile march, at WISSANT.	

R M Pringle
Lt Col. Comdg 171 Bde. RFA.

Army Form C. 2118.

WAR DIARY
or
INTELLIGENCE SUMMARY
(Erase heading not required.)

A/91 RFA Dec 15/16.

Place	Date	Hour	Summary of Events and Information	Remarks and references to Appendices
EWERDINGHE	Dec 1-15		Battery in billets under Lt.Col. Paterson, Centre Group. Named Truck Warfare. Vacates gun positions on Dec 15/16; leaves 1st position occupied; now to Elverdinghe with British line Northwards. Proceeds to WATOU West area.	
	15			

Rumsden Bdr
Officer Comdg A/91 RFA

Army Form C. 2118.

WAR DIARY
or
INTELLIGENCE SUMMARY   B/121.
(Erase heading not required.)

December 1916.

Place	Date	Hour	Summary of Events and Information	Remarks and references to Appendices
ELVERDINGHE.	1916 Dec. 1-15.	—	Weather on Reconnaissance on battery, under Lt-Col. Paterson, and Centre Group. No weather protection. Normal Trench Warfare.	
	15.		Relieved by 39th Div. on night 14/15 & 15/16 Dec. Proceeded West area ASWATON	

Rhodes m
for Major Cmdg. B/121 R.F.A.

WAR DIARY
or
INTELLIGENCE SUMMARY

Army Form C. 2118

Place	Date	Hour	Summary of Events and Information	Remarks and references to Appendices
	1st to 15th		In action as before.	
	14th and 15th		Relieved by A/174.	
	15th to 28th		In rest at WATOU.	
	29th		Marched to WULVERDINGHE - NORDAUSQUES.	
	30th		" - WISSANT for training.	
	31st		" - training.	
	21st		2/Lt Rimmer went on leave.	
	17th		2/Lt Stern and Cpl. Bannister to 2nd Army artillery school.	
	31st		2/Lt Thompson went on leave.	

Officers:
Capt B.McKg. Queen
2/Lt W.C. Stern
2/Lt J.H. Rimmer
" G. Thompson
" A. Rittle

[signature]

WAR DIARY or INTELLIGENCE SUMMARY

Army Form C. 2118

D/12.

(1st R.W.F.)

Place	Date 1916 December	Hour	Summary of Events and Information	Remarks and references to Appendices
YPRES I.2.C.9.2. 3 gun in action N.12.4.4	1.		Very foggy. No firing.	12 midnight heavy battle bombardment & raid on Left Battalion front. Fired 60 rounds rifle lines installation. All quiet 1 am
	2.	2.45 pm	Foggy. Observation beyond front trench impossible. Fired 2 rounds on No 1 gun Night firing (C.14.c.7/20) to Test ESSEN Barrage.	
	3.	10.53 am	Poor light. Enemy shelled front line in C14.c.rd with 4.7cm at 11.30 am - 20 rounds. Fired 20 rounds at C.7.c.6.4. - "BOMBARD"	with good results
		11.6 am	" 20 " " - MOLTKE Redoubt - "MOLTKE"	
		11.24 am	" 10 " " - C.14.B.5.5. - "MINNIE"	
		3 pm	" 15 " " - PILKEM MILL and on Maj Schwaben to check reported after eight days of fog	
	4.		Light very fair. Considerable movement by 3rd Div. Infantry in vicinity of FRASCATI. This is very unusual in daylight on clear days.	Smoke curling fum
	5.		Good light. 1 german seen walking EAST at C.14.a.5.2.	
			Our S.O.S on MOLTKE Redoubt.	
		12.8 pm	Fired 30 rounds at C.C.C.6.7. - "BOMBARD"	Excellent bursts
		12.24 pm	do " " "	
		3.31 pm	do " " "	
		3.50 pm	" 30 " " MOLTKE Redoubt - "MOLTKE"	Rifle too far for Observation
		3.54 pm	" 8 " " C.14.B.3.5 - "MINNIE"	
	6.		Enemy retaliated heavily (12 noon to 1 pm) on BRIQUE road in vicinity of 0/121 alternating position with salvoes of 10.5 cm. Ken. Good detonations. Large craters. about 60 rounds fired.	
		11.50 am	Fired 8 rounds at C.14.B.3.5 - "MINNIE" - Test S.O.S.	
		2.5 pm	3 on Night line -	
		2 pm	Enemy shelled cross road & vicinity of TURCO FARM with 4.7cm. (30 rounds)	

Army Form C. 2118

WAR DIARY
or
INTELLIGENCE SUMMARY
(Erase heading not required.)

D/121

Instructions regarding War Diaries and Intelligence Summaries are contained in F.S. Regs., Part II. and the Staff Manual respectively. Title Pages will be prepared in manuscript.

Place	Date	Hour	Summary of Events and Information	Remarks and references to Appendices
	7.		Very misty till 2pm. Then much safer visible in vicinity of C.14.a.7.3. Quiet day	
	8.		Foggy. Observation impossible. Quiet day.	
	9.		Misty rain. A few light at times. Moderate Southerly wind.	
		11:30 am	Fired 3 rounds on PILCKEM MILL — Re-registration	
		11:45 am	" 6 " C.1.E.93 — do. Enemy Battery positron E Pilht.
		12 noon	" 11 " FORTIN 17 — do.
		12:45pm	" 12 " FARM 14 — do.
		4:30pm	" 12 " C.14. E.3.5. — "MINNIE"
		4:35pm	" 12 " do. — do.
	10.		No 3 gun brought into action at night.
			Good light.
		11:26 am	Fired 11 rounds at PILCKEM MILL — Registration of No 3 gun.
		1:27pm	" 5 " C.14. a 7.2.0. — " Test ESSEN Barrage
		4pm	" 12 " C.14. E.3.5. — "MINNIE".
		4:12pm	" 12 " C.14. a 8.6. — "MINNIE EATING".
	11.	1:5pm	" 10 " PILCKEM MILL — Registration of No 3 gun. Balloon Rg. Considerable mutual aircraft activity — got 3 rounds (Medium T.M) fell between FUSILIER FARM & C.14. E.95 in answer.

WAR DIARY
or
INTELLIGENCE SUMMARY
(Erase heading not required.)

Army Form C. 2118

Place	Date	Hour	Summary of Events and Information	Remarks and references to Appendices
YPRES.	12.		Rain & sleet. Observation handicapped by Cloud visibility	
		3:30pm	Service of National Prayer & Intercession & Notice at gunposition – Rev. Kidd.	
			R.C. & Scotch in command of Inferior Potters (C/119) variable gunposition	
			& alternate position & were tightly planed with the firemen.	
		13.	Brilliant R.A.T. & calm.	
		14.	Right Section relieved by C/119. Visits to O.P. by C.O.C.'s & CR.A.s	
			18th Div., 39th Div., to gunposition by C.R.A.S. and	
		15.	Left Section relieved by C/119. Wagon line marched to WATOU.	
			Lorry transport for Gunners	
	31/12/16.			

[Signatures]
Major R.F.A.
Capt. R.F.A.
cmdg. D/12 Bde R.F.A.

War Diary D/121.
(1/12/16 — 15/12/16.)

Adjutant,
121st Bde RFA

Army Form C. 2118.

WAR DIARY
or
INTELLIGENCE SUMMARY

(Erase heading not required.)

131st Brigade R.F.A.
January 1917.

YR/3

Place	Date	Hour	Summary of Events and Information	Remarks and references to Appendices
	1st to 9th		The Brigade was in training at WISSANT near Calais, where training (Riding & Shelter gun drill etc) was carried out on the sands, which greatly added to the efficiency of all ranks.	
	10th		The Brigade marched from WISSANT to NORDAUSQUES, much very cold & wet weather.	
	11th		marched to LEDERZEELE.	
	12th		marched from LEDERZEELE to HONDKERQUE, where the Brigade remained in rest until 17th & 18th	
	17th 18th		The Brigade relieved the Centre Group (on Left Group) of the 29th Division at BRIELEN and ELVERDINGHE.	

WAR DIARY
or
INTELLIGENCE SUMMARY

Army Form C. 2118.

Place	Date	Hour	Summary of Events and Information	Remarks and references to Appendices
	30th		The 121st Brigade Headquarters moved to Centre Group HQrs at TROIS TOURS CHATEAU, under the command of Lieut Colonel H.G. Pringle D.S.O., R.F.A. "B" and "C" Batteries were attached "A" going to Left Group and "C" to the Right Group. It has been noticed that since on left the enemy is the time of taking over again the enemy has become much more aggressive. The enemy at about 1.40am attempted to raid the trenches on our extreme right which was covered by the Right Group. The firing was excellent and thereby prevented the enemy from reaching our trenches.	

J.F. Moore (?) Lt Col R.F.A.
Cmdg 121 Bde R.F.A.

Army Form C. 2118

WAR DIARY
or
INTELLIGENCE SUMMARY

(Erase heading not required.)

O/121 January 1918

Place	Date	Hour	Summary of Events and Information	Remarks and references to Appendices
WISSANT	1st		Training	
	6th			
	9th		Marched back to NORDAUSQUES	
	10th		" " LEDERZEELE	
	11th		" " HOUTKERQUE	
	12th		Lt STONE rejoined from 2nd Army School	
	13th		Lt NOBLE went on leave	
	14th		19611 B.S.M. ARDEN joined from Base	
	"		Bt X went into action } in old position at YPRES	
	17th		Cx and Lx " }	
	"		hui A rot 2.2	
	18th		Major B/IIn	
			M/C H.MOORE joined from B/IIn	
	25th		Considerable Enemy artillery activity	
	19th			Officers present
	-31st			Major B Stephenson
				Capt O.A.C. Stone
				Lt 9/Lt Rimmer
				Lt Thompson
				" " Noble
				" Horth
				" Capt Moore
				B/Sm Arden

B Stephenson
Major R.F.A.
Comdg O/121

Army Form C. 2118.

WAR DIARY
or
INTELLIGENCE SUMMARY

121 A.A. R.A
February 1917.

Vol 14

Place	Date	Hour	Summary of Events and Information	Remarks and references to Appendices
Trois Tours	Feb. 1917.		During February 121 A.A. Headquarters were still commanding Cate Group 361st D.A. From Trois Tours, Brielen. Batteries in the Group were B/121, D/121, A/B + D/119; C/177 and C/177 (How) front of 4th line. A/121 with the 4th Group, C/177 with the Right.	
	3rd		C/177 (How.) came into the position at B.21.b.4.6., last occupied by A/121 after the Division went out of front in December 1916. The "Circus" (Heavy Artillery) was a 24hrs corps front during the 1st half 4th month. Pas Flessant Boesinghe A.P.A place in co-operation with them. Hostile artillery continued active. Specially on Gun positions & Places in rear of the line; B/119 was again shelled; B/121 and D/121 have also been shelled; Lieut F. Arnold and Gunner Cockridge of D/121, were the 7th killing Gunn & nailing Lugage respectively for welcome amongst on the latter occasion. B/121 cooperated with Heavy Artillery in bombardment of hostile front defences	
Boesinghe	8th		Krupp Salvo bombarded by H.A. 301st D.A of Cate Group cooperated.	
	4th		Bombardment by Cate Group of C.T.C.	G.O.C. attached

Army Form C. 2118.

WAR DIARY
or
INTELLIGENCE SUMMARY
(Erase heading not required)

121 Bde. R.F.A. February 1917

Place	Date	Hour	Summary of Events and Information	Remarks and references to Appendices
TROIS TOURS	8th		Lt. Col. H.G. PRINGLE DSO. RFA proceeds on leave. Lt.Col. ARCHDALE DSO. RFA (adj. 77/(1)Bde RFA) taken over command of Bde. Pringe.	
	14th		Ammunition Warrain issued at for Bn. howis. redried from 1000 rds per gun (10 pdr.) to 403 rds. 4.5 Hows to 274 rounds.	
	17th & 18th		Raw 5.4.H. Buff. Carries out Zero hour 319 am. 10th. Cash. Bringe programme attacked. Bombardment by H.A. and 35th DA. take place 6 days prevain on (1) KRUPP Salient (2) C7 c and d. Uncicallis at C14 a 3.4 6 Tm. s and 10 h.Sr. (proves fin at 2v0 b1 fm: works [C12 77]; also, on front, as C7 c 67, and opposite HIGH COMMAND by flight Group.	O.O. attached
	18 - 19		Throughout day and night intermitten bursts of fire kept up sr course to her intervals on Enemy's communication tracks, tripede a suspected German relief. Our Rang Y.P.Or. in armer between bursts of fire.	
	24/5.		Uthing Shelling at 3am. 25th. The Bury raided on tucks near 5th EACING TRENCH capture a machine Sun. Their were only a for 2 or 3 mina bs. Casti Sints Saraigs	

It not the front.

Army Form C. 2118.

WAR DIARY
or
INTELLIGENCE SUMMARY
12. BdA RFA Feb 1917
(Erase heading not required.)

Place	Date	Hour	Summary of Events and Information	Remarks and references to Appendices
TROIS TOURS	26.			
	27.		At 3 pm Lt. Col. W.E. RUDKIN D.S.O. R.A. took command of Right Group, relieving Lt. Col. Howland-Roberts who is in Cmd + till his Successor 12 Bde H.Q. remain full known at TROIS TOURS.	
	28th		Water huts. Six Ration wagon huts have been taken from the 55th Divl WL. and they were occupied by these old water huts at HANNHOEK, hand write to la zones.	

Rudkin Lt Col RA
Afterwards Lt Col RA [on leave].
for O.C. 12 BdA RFA.
1.3.17.

WAR DIARY or INTELLIGENCE SUMMARY

C/121 February 1917 Army Form C. 2118

Place	Date	Hour	Summary of Events and Information	Remarks and references to Appendices
	17th		Same position at YPRES.	
	19th		Lieut. R.E.L. MABEY joined.	
	"		" proceeded to hospital.	
	26th		436 Stella Battery. A. Sgt. F. GIBSON slightly wounded.	
	27th		No. 1487 Sgt. G. RICHARDS left to proceed to Cadet School with a view to a commission. A prad died of shooting this month. Officers present:— Major D.C.C. Stephenson Captain W.A.C. Stone Lieut J.H. Rimmer " J. Thompson " Mr. A. Smith " C.H. Moore " R.E.L. Mabey	

D. Stephenson
Major
Comdg C/121

19611 B.S.M. Arden
1961 B.S.M. Arden

S E C R E T.   OPERATION ORDER No.15.

The following action will take place tomorrow the 4th inst –

B/119.   1 Section.   C.2.c.1.6½. – C.2.a.3½.2.
opening fire at 9.30 a.m., firing 1 salvo followed
by 2 rounds gun fire, at irregular intervals averaging
half an hour till 4 p.m. (H.E.)

D/119.   C.2.c.2½.1½ – C.2.c.½.6.
50 rounds per gun lasting from 12 noon till 4 p.m.

D/121.   C.2.c.2½.1½ – C.2.c.6½.2½.
50 rounds per gun lasting from 12 noon till 4 p.m.

                                    Lieut. Colonel R.F.A.
3-2-17.   Commanding CENTRE GROUP R.F.A.

SECRET.   OPERATION ORDER No. 21

A RAID by the 14th R.W.F. will take place about the 17th inst. Point of Entry - C.14.a.3½.4.
The Party will penetrate as far as C.14.a.4½.5¾. and blocking parties will be placed at the following points :-
C.14.a.5.4., CAKE SUPPORT, C.14.a.2¼.5., C.14.a.4.2. both in front line.
The Trench Tramway will also be blocked each side of the C.T.

PRELIMINARY BOMBARDMENT.

The Heavy Artillery will bombard the front line between CAESARS NOSE and KRUPP FARM, paying particular attention to Machine Gun emplacements and between FORTIN 17 and C.7.c.6.7½. Exact date of Bombardment will be notified later. D/121. (& ~~C~~) will each put 50 rds. daily on and after the 13th. inst. into C.7.c.6.7½.

WIRE CUTTING.

The wire at Point of Entry will be cut by the Trench Mortars. Registration will take place on the 12th. and cutting will commence on the 13th. Covering fire will be supplied by B/119. An 18 pdr. gun from B/121. placed behind RIVOLI FARM will supplement the work of the Trench Mortars if necessary. Wire will also be cut at C.7.c.6.7½. by B/121. and by the RIGHT GROUP at some point in front of HIGH COMMAND REDOUBT.

ARTILLERY PROGRAMME.

Artillery Support will consist of a 3 minute Bombardment of the Front Line and Support Lines lifting on to the Barrage lines as the Raid Progresses.
Detailed time-table as below :-
00 - 03. Front Line and Support Line Bombardment. Box Barrage.
03 - 06. Support Line Bombardment. Box Barrage.
06 - ~~30~~. Box Barrage.

SWITCH.

The guns firing on the Support trenches continue fire 3 minutes after the Assault of the Front Line. This period may have to be extended as it depends on the state of the trenches. Batteries concerned should therefore be prepared for such an alteration which will be notified to them on the Day.

(2)

BOMBARDMENT.

0.00 - 0.03.

(1) Front Line.

B/119.	1 Section.	C.14.a.5½.1½. - C.14.a.4.2½. ✓
	Enfilade Section.	C.14.a.4¼.2. - C.14.a.3¼.4. ✓
B/121.	1 Section.	C.14.a.3½.4. - C.14.a.2¾.4¾. ✓
A/119.		C.14.a.2¾.4¾. - C.14.a.1.7. ✓

(2) Support and Communication trenches.

RIGHT GROUP.	4 guns. CAKE LANE.	C.14.a.7.3. - C.14.a.7½.7½. ✓
B/121.	1 Section.	C.14.a.5.4½. - C.14.a.4.5. —5½. ✓
	1 ,,	C.14.a.8.7½. - C.14.a.5.8½. ✓
B/119.	1 ,,	C.14.a.1.7. - C.14.a.2½.8. ✓
C/277.	1 gun.	C.14.a.2½.8. ✓
	1 Section.	C.14.a.5¾.8. - C.14.a.5.9½. ✓
	1 gun.	C.8.c.2.2½. - ✓
	Forward Sec. 5mm	C.13.b.8½.8. — C.14.a.1.7.

Hows.-		
D/119.	1 How.	C.14.a.8.0. - C.14.a.9.0. C.14.a.8.0 ✓
	1 How.	C.14.a.6.2½.
	1 How.	C.14.a.1½.6.
D/121.	2 Hows.	KOLN FARM.
	1 How.	C.14.a.4.6.
	1 How.	C.13.b.8½.8.

SWITCH.

03.06.
B/119.   1 Section.   C.14.a.1.7. - C.14.a.2½.8.
         Enfilade Section. C.14.a.5.3. - C.14.a.5.4¾.
         1 Section.   C.14.a.5½.1½. - C.14.a.7.2½.
B/121.   1 Section.   C.14.a.4.6. - C.14.a.3½.7.
         1   ,,   C.14.a.7½.7½. - C.14.a.(5.9.) 5¾.8
         1   ,,   C.14.a.5.4½. - C.14.a.4.5½.
A/119.   C.14.a.3½.7. - C.14.a.1.9½.
C/277.   1 Section.   C.14.a.5¾.8. - C.14.a.5.9½.
         1   ,,   C.14.a.2½.8. - ~~C.14.a.5.9.~~ C.8.c.1½.0.

Hows.

D/119.   2 Hows.   C.14.a.8.0. - C.14.a.9.0.
         1 How.   C.14.a.6.2½.
         1 How.   C.13.b.8½.8.
D/121.   2 Hows.   KOLN FARM.
         1 ,,   C.14.a.2½.8.
         1 ,,   C.13.b.8½.8.

RIGHT GROUP. (as above)

HEAVY ARTILLERY. (throughout operations.)

Howitzers –
Trench Junction.   C.14.b.6¾.9½.
    ”   ”c   C.8.c.9¼.3½.
                      MACKENSEN FARM.
                      AEOLIAN FARM.
Trench Junction.   C.8.c.0.8½.

2.6" Hows. from ELVERDINGHE direction :-

0.00 – 10.03   C.14.a.5.8½. – C.8.c.2.2½.
0.03 to end of Operation. Concentrate on C.8.c.2.2½.

(60 pdrs.   C.14.a.1.9½. – C.8.c.2.2½.   ) *on counter Battery*
                  C.14.a.5.9. – C.8.c.2.2½.   ) *work*

TRENCH MORTARS.

4 Medium Trench Mortars to join in preliminary Bombardment engaging
C.14.a.3½.4.
at 0.03 – 10.05 two switch to C.14.a.4.2½.
                two switch to C.14.a.1½.6.

Also at least 2 medium should engage KRUPP SALIENT and ESSEN FM *& retirement*
if it can be reached and two on C.13.b.8.8.

COMMUNICATIONS.

1 Officer of B/119. to be with Commander of RAID
with Visual Signalling to HUDDERSFIELD O.P. 1 Officer of A/319.
to be at LANCASHIRE FM with O.C. 14th R.W.F. with lamp communication
with A/119 O.P.

BARRAGE.

RIGHT GROUP – 4 Guns. (as above)
B/119. Enfilade Section. Search CHEMIN AVENUE for 200 yards.
               from   C.14.a.8¾.7.
      1 Section.   C.14.a.1.7. – C.14.a.2½.8.
      1   ,,   C.14.a.5.1½. – C.14.a.7.2½.
A/119. 1   ,,   C.14.a.3.7½. – C.14.a.2.8¾.
      4 guns.   C.14.a.2½.8. – C.14.a.5.9.
B/121. 6 guns.   C.14.a.7½.7½. – C.14.a.5.9.
C/277. (as above)

Hows. as above except :- 1 How. D/119. on C.14.a.6.2½. changes to
                                              C.14.a.7.2½.

RATE OF FIRE -

(1) BOMBARDMENT.
       B/121.   5 rounds per gun per minute.
       A/119.   5   "   "   "
       B/119. less section on
              C.14.a.1.7. - 2½.8. 5 rds per gun per minute.
Remainder - 3 rounds per gun per minute.
All Hows. - 3 rounds per gun per minute.

(2) SWITCH.
       B/119. Enfilade Section.   5 rounds per gun per minute.
       B/121. Forward Section.   5   "   "   "
       A/119. 1 Section on C.14.a.3½.7. - C.14.a.2½.8.
                           - 5 rounds per gun per minute.
Remainder - 3 rounds per gun per minute.
Hows.   - 3 rounds per gun per minute.

(3) BARRAGE.
       All 18 pdrs. 3 rounds per gun per minute.
       Howitzers.   3 rounds per gun per 2 minutes.

4 (CHANGE)

SECRET.

AMENDMENTS & ADDITIONS to OPERATION ORDER No. 21.

(Amendments and additions are marked in RED) None

BOMBARDMENT.

(1) Front Line.
C/277. 1 Section.   C.13.b.9½.7¾. – C.14.a.½.7¼.
(2) Support & Communication Trenches.
LEFT GROUP. 1 Gun. C.14.a.6.7½. }
             1 gun. C.14.a.2½.6.   } Enfilade from C.25.d.

Hows.
LEFT GROUP. 1 How. C.14.a.5.9.
             1 How. C.8.c.1.0.

SWITCH.

B/119. 1 Section.   C.14.a.5½.1½. – C.14.a.7.2½.
B/121. 1 Section.   C.14.a.4½.6½. – C.14.a.3½.7.
        1   "   C.14.a.7½.7½. – C.14.a.5½.8½.
        1   "   C.14.a.1½.4½. – C.14.a.4.5½.
C/277. 1 Section.   C.14.a.5½.8½. – C.14.a.5.9½.
        1   "   C.13.b.9½.7¾. – C.14.a.½.7¼. as before.
        Forward gun.   C.8.c.2.2½.
LEFT GROUP. 1 Enfilade gun. C.14.a.4½.7½.
             1   "   "   C.14.a.6.7½. as before.

Hows.
B/119. 1 How.   C.14.a.5½.8½. as before.
        1 How.   C.14.a.6.2½.   } as type 1
        1 How.   C.13.b.9.8.   }
LEFT GROUP. 1 How. C.14.a.5.9. as before.
             1 How. C.8.c.1.0.   as before.

BARRAGE.

B/119. 1 Section.   C.14.a.5½.1½. – C.14.a.7.2½.
C/277. 1   "   C.14.a.5½.8½. – C.14.a.4½.9½.
        Remainder as above.
LEFT GROUP. 1 Gun. C.8.c.1.0. as above.
             1 Gun. C.8.c.3½.4.
             Hows. as above except 2 Hows. B/119. on C.14.a.6.2½.
             change to C.14.a.7.2½.

TRENCH MORTARS.

Time 0.00 to 0.04. 1 T.M. (firing delay fuze) C.14.a.5½.1½.
Searching back to C.14.a.5½.12.
Time 0.00 to end of Operations, 2 Mortars on C.7.c.23.98.
O.C. 113th Infantry Brigade is arranging for STOKES Mortars to
engage Hostile Front line at CAESARS NOSE & KRUPP SALIENT.

S E C R E T.

ADDITION TO OPERATION ORDER No.21.

(IV) "CHANGE" — This order will be given when the Raiding Party leave the Enemy trenches to return to our own lines.—

C/273.	5 guns.	C.13.b.8½.6.	— C.14.a.06.72.
A/119.	6 guns.	C.14.a.06.72.	— C.14.a.27.50.
B/121.	6 guns.	C.14.a.27.50.	— C.14.a.39.27.
B/119.	6 guns.	C.14.a.39.27.	— C.14.a.55.15.

RIGHT GROUP. 4 guns. C.14.a.55.15. — C.14.a.68.03.

LEFT GROUP. 2 guns. C.14.a.68.03. — C.14.a.8.0.

RATE OF FIRE — 3 rounds per gun per minute. Time shrapnel.

HOWITZERS — as in bombardment.

RATE OF FIRE — 3 rounds per gun per 2 minutes.

MAJOR. R.F.A.
Commanding CENTRE GROUP R.F.A.

16-2-17.

S E C R E T.

AMENDMENTS (2) to OPERATION ORDER No.21.

BOMBARDMENT.

(ii) LEFT GROUP. substitute :- 2 guns C.14.a.5.3. - C.14.a.62.20.
C/277. 1 gun - substitute C.14.a.2½.8.

Hows. - LEFT GROUP. 1 How. - for C.14.a.5.9. substitute C.14.a.5¾.8¼.

SWIACH.

D/119. 1 How. C.14.a.5¾.8¼. erase "as before".

BOX BARRAGE.

0.06 - "CHANGE" (order from Group)

B/119. 1 Section (that previously mentioned in "Amendments")
substitute - C.14.a.50.16. - C.14.a.54.22.

                                                Major R.F.A.
                                    Commanding CENTRE GROUP R.F.A.

16-2-17.

Confidential

Army Form C. 2118.

WAR DIARY

INTELLIGENCE SUMMARY — H.Q. 1st Bde. R.H.A. — March 1916.

Vol 15

Place	Date	Hour	Summary of Events and Information	Remarks and references to Appendices
TROIS TOURS	March 1916.			
	1st onwards		Brigade HQ. still at/action, and still at TROIS TOURS. Minimum number of Telephonists still employed in mining (telephone exchange) to 4 batteries of Rifle Grps. Men at "Z.12." Position in Belgian lines. Rifle battery 1st Div Grps. B/1st in Dunkirk. C/1st near YPRES. D/1st on — YPRES, under Rifle Grps.	See Special War Diaries.
	17th		Rifle battn relieves 12th Bde + 119 Bde at St Smith. 12 Bde. Canadian	
	20th		B/1st heavily shelled at position in B5G. Two men killed.	
	22nd	6 pm	Do Battery again comes into action at "Cabi Grp" — this time only 3 batteries. B/1st, B/119, D/119. Grp commander Major Bg.Woods (B/119)	
	22/23 (night)		Raid by Enemy on Rifle Grp front. Bn Batteries support Rifle front in barrage "KRUPP – WECO".	
	28th		B/1st moved into another position at B.21.6 (4 guns), 2 guns still in "EVERDINGHE WOOD".	
			Lieut. Col. H.G. Pringh D.S.O. R.F.A., who had commanded the Brigade since the end of 1915 having shrewd of strength, now goes sick in England. He had been away more than 6 weeks; the Brigade was commanded in his absence by Major M.D. Townsend R.F.A. (A/or.) Their Col. G.P. MacClellan D.S.O. R.F.A. assumes command 1/15.	

2353 Wt. W.2544/1454 700,000 5/15 D.D.&L. A.D.S.S./Forms/C. 2118.

Army Form C. 2118.

WAR DIARY
INTELLIGENCE SUMMARY.
(Erase heading not required.)

War Diary 121st Bde R.F.A. - march 1917

Place	Date	Hour	Summary of Events and Information	Remarks and references to Appendices
TROIS TOURS	March 19th		Brigade, and also of the Centre Group	
	28th		Lieut. DENOE (orderly officer) appointed adjutant 77th Bde RFA (Capt. Anstuck). Major NOBLE (C/121) takes his place as adjutant.	
	29th		Our Heavy Trench Mortar replies on the left; enemy fire supplied by our two 10½" Batteries	
	29/30 (night)		P.O.S. light group; fire opened which continued for over 1 hour. 9 batts including parts of groups on Right group front.	
			A/121 and A/115 started into charge positions: A/121 comes to DAWSON'S CORNER, into Right Group –	
	30/31 and 31/1		W-62. G.P. MacLellan takes command of Right Group in Br. R.J. Reid's absence. Major FP. WYE (D/115) – MacLellans – – Anstir	
	31st		New batteries positions. No much incident during the month; HQ. wagon lines only twice twice work at wagon line as usual.	
			practically completed.	
			Major J.Anstuck (B)/115 late Y/B R.R.E.A.	

31.3.17

G.McLellan
Lieut. Colonel, R.F.A.
Commanding.
121st Brigade, R.F.A.

WAR DIARY
or
INTELLIGENCE SUMMARY A/121 R.F.A.

(Erase heading not required.)

Army Form C. 2118

Place	Date	Hour	Summary of Events and Information	Remarks and references to Appendices
	March.			
	13th.		The Battery still in action at ZIZI, near ZUYDSCHOOTE. Only 8 rounds were fired during the month. All the time was occupied in building strong concrete gun pits.	
	18th.		The KEMMELBEKE rose 6 feet and the position was flooded, especially the left section. The Battery was inspected by the Corps Commander.	
	25th & 30th		Four gunners wounded by a stray 77cm shell.	
	29th.		The Belgians in front of us made 2 raids near STEEN STRAATE; several Germans were killed & 18 prisoners taken. One gunner, attached from B.A.C., was wounded.	
	30th & 31st		On the evenings of 30th & 31st we relieved A/119 R.F.A. at DAWSON'S Corner. Our forward wagon line at STEENTJE Farm remains where it is at present.	

(M.S.) Greene
Major
Cmdg 121 Bde
R.F.A.

31-3-17.

B Battery 121st Brigade R.F.A.
War Diary — March 1917

1st March 1917 — Battery - Left flank battery of Right Group, commanded by Lieut: Col: C.E. Rudkin D.S.O. R.F.A.
Battery Position B.15.b.7.7.
About 11.a.m The enemy commenced shelling this Battery position with 15.c.m., & after registering continued to shell the position with 77m.m 10.5 c.m & 15 c.m guns, till about 4 p.m. Approximately 300 rounds were fired. Damage done - one side of ammunition dump blown in. One detachment dug-out blown in. One gun out of action, being struck in the muzzle by a splinter. Communications reestablished & battery in action again at 8 p.m.

2.3.17 — Battery fired 40 rounds on enemy front line in retaliation. Position inspected by Corps Artillery Adviser.

3.3.17 — Fired at Working party, & on front line in retaliation.

4.3.17 — Registered fresh targets.

5-7.3.17 — Fired on registered targets.

8-9. — Registered fresh retaliation points on front line as ordered by Group. & fired on Working party. Strong wind & snow squalls.

10.3.17 — Checked registrations.

11.3.17 — Fired on front line in retaliation.

12.3.17 — Registered Trench Junctions C.7.a.4.3 & C.7.d.9.8½

13.3.17	Fired at a dispersed Working party.
14.3.17	Fired on Front Line & registered PILCKEM CROSS ROADS.
	Battery commanders conference at Right Group Headquarters.
15.3.17	Fired at Working parties
	Hostile aircraft fairly active.
16.3.17	Various targets engaged.
17.3.17	Fired on Trench Junctions, and on New Tramway observed & reported.
	Light very good & much movement seen & reported.
18.3.17	Several Working parties observed & fired on. – dispersing same.
	Hostile Balloons up. – bearings taken.
19.3.17	Much new work observed & reported.
20.3.17	10 a.m to 12 noon Enemy registered Battery position with 10.5 c.m.
	2 p.m to 4 p.m. Enemy shelled the position with 15 c.m How desultory, which broke into gun fire for an hour deliberate shelling. A great number of blinds, or apparently gas shells were used.
	Damage. – One dug-out sustained a direct hit. Direct hit on ammunition dump.
	Casualties :- Two men killed.
	Approximate No. of rounds fired 500.
	Communications were reestablished & battery in action about 9 p.m.
21.3.17	Hostile Artillery active.
	Many Working parties observed & reported. Hostile Balloons up.
	Battery came under orders of Centre

21.3.17 Group commanded by Major A.E. Wood, M.C R.F.A.

22.3.17 About 4.6 am S.O.S rockets observed, and battery opened fire on S.O.S. lines.

G.D. Thomas Capt R.A.
O.C. B/121 Bde R.F.A.

WAR DIARY
or
INTELLIGENCE SUMMARY

C/121.
March 1917.

Date	Hour	Summary of Events and Information	Remarks
4th		Still in action in outskirts of Ypres.	
		2nd Lieut C.W. FITZHERBERT R.F.A. (S.R.) joined.	
11th		" C.H. MOORE went to 2nd Army Artillery School.	
18th		68232 Sgt. J.H. AVIS promoted B.S.M. and posted to 119 Bde.	
26th		2nd Lieut R.E.L. MABEY on course at Div. Gas School.	
29th		M.A.P NOBLE transferred to B.de H.Q. as orderly Officer.	
28th		C.W. FITZHERBERT taken on strength.	
		Prepared to support Raid in MORTELDJE – failure.	
		The Battery was in action at night, firing on S.O.S. and barrage lines many times a week.	

Major D.L. Stephenson
Capt W.L. Sermon
Lieut G.H. Rimmer
" J. Thompson
" C.H. Moore
" C.W. Fitzherbert
" R.E.L Mabey (attached)

19611 B.S.M F. Arden.

D.L. Stephenson
Major R.F.A.
Comdy C/121 Bde

WAR DIARY or INTELLIGENCE SUMMARY

Army Form C. 2118

(Erase heading not required.)

Place	Date	Hour	Summary of Events and Information	Remarks and references to Appendices
the field	21/3/17	2.30pm	Fired 8 Rounds at C.2.C.8½.3½. with satisfactory results.	
"		3.15pm	" 1st Rds. at C. 1st. a. 4ff. 5ff. New work, 3 direct hits.	
"		5pm	" 2nd Rds. at C. 1st. B.O.1. +C. 1st. B.2.1.	
"	23/3/17	9.55am	Enemy shelled position in vicinity with 15 cm gun – 27 Rds.	
"		12.15pm	do	200 Rds.
"		2pm	do	with 77 mm gun – 100 Rds
"		3.40pm to 3.55pm	do with 10.5 cm gun	50 Rds.
"	24/3/17	1.40pm to 5.25pm	do with 15 cm gun	30 Rds.
"	25/3/17	10 am	Fired 2f Rounds on C.14.a.60.85 + C.14.a. 5½.8½ by order of Group with satisfactory result.	
"	26/3/17	1.50pm		
"	27/3/17	11.30pm	Fired 12 Rounds on C.2.C.8½.3½. with satisfactory results.	
"	"	10.30pm	Enemy shelled position with 77 mm gun. 20 Rounds.	

WAR DIARY
or
INTELLIGENCE SUMMARY
(Erase heading not required.)

Army Form C. 2118

Place	Date	Hour	Summary of Events and Information	Remarks and references to Appendices
Observ Posts	29/3/17	6 pm	Fires on. C.14.a.8½.5. with good results. 10 Rounds.	
"	30/3/17	3.26 p/m	Fired on C.14.B.40.25. C.14.B.05.10. C.14.a.8.0. C.14.a.35.40. S.O.S. Ranged. 6 Rounds.	
"	30/3/17 4-8 p/m		Fired on C.14.a.6.0.85. ½C.14.a.2½.8½. 32 Rounds. Group order	
"	"	4.18 p/m	Fired on C.1st.6.40.25. C.1st.6.05.10. C.14.a.8.0. C.14.a.35.40.	
"	"	4.36 p/m	Group order. 68 Rounds.	
"	"	5-8 p/m	Fired on C.15.a.0.2½. to C.15.a.3.2½ 82 Rounds Group orders.	
"	"	5.6 p/m	do do 80 Rounds.	
"	"	5.20 p/m	Fired on dugouts and bank of phone. at C.20.9.7. 3 hits on the house.	
"	"	5.20 p/m	Fired on large concrete dugout at C.2.C.6½.4½.	
"	31/3/17	3.50 p/m	Fired on C.30.8½.3½. with satisfactory results.	
"	"	6.5 p/m	" on C.14.a.8.0. C.14.6.4.2¾ C.14.6.½.1. C.14.a.3.2½. with good result.	

31st March 1917

[signature]
Major R.F.A.
Comd of 2/121. Bde RFA

121 Bgde RA Army Form C. 2118

Vol 16

WAR DIARY
or
INTELLIGENCE SUMMARY
(Erase heading not required.)

Place	Date	Hour	Summary of Events and Information	Remarks and references to Appendices
In the Field	1/4/17	8.5 am	Fired 25 Rounds on C.8.d.95.10. Group orders	
		10 am	Retired of Rt position on BELLEWARDE BEEK commenced.	
	2/4/17	5.30 Nm		
"	3/4/17	3.10 pm	Fired 16 Rounds on C.8.C.30. Group orders satisfactory round.	
"	3/4/17	11.10 pm	Fired 40 Rounds on Night fires, Group orders	
	6/4/17		Inspection of O.P and organisation by Info Commander	
"	5/4/17	11 am	Fired 4 Rounds on 16. 2.C. 8½. 3½. to Empty Guns nearest Gunners	
"	13/4/17	3.45 pm to 3.30 pm	Fired 13 Rounds on C.2.C.8½. 3½. Configuration of Guns nearness from I.O.M satisfactory results	
"	14/4/17	4.10 am	Fired 19 Shots at GENERAL FARM.	
"	"	4.15 pm	Fired 14 Rds at Probable O.P. (Coupole very noticeable today) on C.1.a. 3½. 8. on edge of BOIS 15. Bracketed but not hit - Frosty wind.	
	7/4/17	11.30 pm	Punitive Rounds, filled B 10.5mm. Row. Row. East. Row. Telephone pit Rut, pit at furtated	
	8/4/17	12.30 am	Garrison dull. YPRES watched town fell.	

Army Form C. 2118

WAR DIARY
or
INTELLIGENCE SUMMARY
(Erase heading not required.)

Instructions regarding War Diaries and Intelligence Summaries are contained in F. S. Regs., Part II. and the Staff Manual respectively. Title Pages will be prepared in manuscript.

Place	Date	Hour	Summary of Events and Information	Remarks and references to Appendices
In the Field	19/4/17	1.30pm	fired 3 rounds on CAESAR'S Fine	
"	"	"	" 6 " " BOIS Fine.	Practice with Box Respirator
"	"	"	" 2 " " G. BARRIER H/se	
"	"	"	" 5 " " SAPEUR H/se.	
"	"	"	" 6 " " House on Railway C.1.d.4.6.	Result satisfactory.
"	"	2.30pm	" 9 " on PILCKEM to check line,	satisfactory result.
"	"	"	" 14 " on NIGHT LINES to check Registration result satisfactory	
"	20/4	10.45am	" 29 " on PERISCOPE H/SE C.2.c.9.7 Suspected O.P.	
"	"	11.30am	" 21 " on 6.14.b. 15.10. New work. Excellent result.	
"	"	3.35pm	" 24 " on 6.8.c. 3.0 & 6.8.c. 20.55. MINNIE SKIPTON order from Group, very good result.	
"	"	4.40pm	" 15 " HINDENBURG FARM. C.8.d.9.5. 2. Order from Group with good result.	

1875 Wt. W593/826 1,000,000 4/15 J.B.C. & A. A.D.S.S./Forms/C. 2118.

WAR DIARY
or
INTELLIGENCE SUMMARY
(Erase heading not required.)

Army Form C. 2118

Place	Date	Hour	Summary of Events and Information	Remarks and references to Appendices
Battlefield	21.4.17	6pm to 7.40pm	Fired 20 Rounds on dug-out near S. edge of Bois 15. Much smoke from 3 huts. Delayed the enemy's dinner quite 2 hours.	
"	25.4.17	10.10pm	Fired 20 Rounds on C.14.6. 1½ . 4½. Order from Group. Football v. R.H.A. Camp depot. Lost 3-1.	
"	23/4/17	2.25pm	Fired 12 Rounds on C.14.6. 05:10. Group order. Very effective	
"	24.4.17	6pm	Fired 22 Rounds on FRONT TRENCH C.14.6.0.1. New Camouflage hurdle seen. 3 sides & a roof, possibly to hide a gap in parapet which exists here. Screen entirely demolished & deposited in "No man's" Land.	
"	"	7pm	Fired 4 rounds on BOIS 15. (S.edge). Smoke from dug-out. Fire extinguished hastily.	
"	25.4.17	4.30pm	Fired 20 Rounds on MOLTKE REDOUBT. Retaliation for T.M. Strafe. Considerable quantity of material dug loose. Group orders	
"	26.4.17	6pm	Fired 20 Rounds on Battery 7.10.5. Group orders. Old gun position enfilade & re-occupied by 29th @ A.	

WAR DIARY
or
INTELLIGENCE SUMMARY

(Erase heading not required.)

Army Form C. 2118.

Place	Date	Hour	Summary of Events and Information	Remarks and references to Appendices
In the Field	26/4/17	1.15 p.m	Fired 15 Rds on P.110 orders from Group.	
"	"	2.45 p.m	" 16 Rounds on SAPEUR HSE C.2.c.2/b.2. Retaliation for T.M. very effective	
"	27/4/17	11.30 p.m	Fired 30 Rounds on P.103. Order from Group	
"	28/4/17	2.40 p.m	Fired 12 Rounds on PILCKEM MILL to check Correction.	
"	"	4.10 p.m	" 36 Rounds. Registration in accordance with B.G.1301	
"	28/4/17	9.40 p.m	Fires 18 on C.14.6. 72:18.	G.1291.
"	"	10.15 p.m	" 18 37:15	
"	"	10.45 p.m	" 24 9.9.	
"	"	11.50 p.m	" 18 65.20.	
"	29/4/17	12.35 a.m	" 24 5.2	
"	"	4.10 a.m	" 18. 35.25	
"	"		Football v. B/122. Won 1-0. 50.47.	

WAR DIARY
or
INTELLIGENCE SUMMARY

(Erase heading not required.)

Army Form C. 2118.

Place	Date	Hour	Summary of Events and Information	Remarks and references to Appendices
In the Field	29/4/17	10.20 a.m	Fired 31 Rounds on C.2.C.8½.8½. Re Calibration. Satisfactory Results.	
"	"	11.10 a.m	" 26 " Registration in accordance with R.F.1201	
"	"	9.30 p.m to 9.50 p.m	Fired 180 Rounds. "Appendix D". R.A.SF.2054. R.F.1201.	
"	30/4/17	12.30 a.m to 12.55 a.m	Fired 90 Rounds. "Appendix E" R.A.SF.2054. R.F.1201.	
"	"	12.55 a.m to 1.20 a.m	Fired 75 Rounds on C.15.a.1.3. orders from FC 30.	
"	30.4.17	4.30 p.m	Fired 8 Rounds on KOLN FARM to check Range for R.G.1201. Satisfactory Results.	
"	"	"	" 8 Rounds. Registration. R.G.1201. Satisfactory results.	
"	1/5/17	1 A.M to 2 A.M	" 330 Rounds. R.A.SF.2054 (Appendix F) R.G.1201	
"	"	4 A.M	" 95 Rounds on NIGHT LINES. S.O.S. call.	

Major R.F.A.
Comdg D/131 Bde

WAR DIARY

Army Form C. 2118.

121 Bde RFA

April 1917.

Place	Date	Hour	Summary of Events and Information	Remarks and references to Appendices
BRIELEN	April 6(?)		TROIS TOURS. Lieut. Col. S.P. MacLellan DSO RFA and 121 AFA HQ. Staff still command 121 Bde. Artillery. Battries of Brigade still located as on the March Diary, A, C and D/121 Bde. guns with Right Group; B/121 alone in Centre Group with B/119 and D/119. Lieut.Col MacLellan and, in his absence, Major F.P. Lorye M.C. and Major D'Eneville M.C. have commanded the group in turn. No front significance the month, which has been quiet. No raids have been carried out either by ourselves on the group front. The Centre Section (returning toward test against salvaging in Group from) of 17 KRRifles, [...] the group has lost the left Battalion (now 113th Battalion) and 113th Battalion in turn. Right Brigade, which has been relieved in turn.	
	29th/30th	At 12-30 a.m. a 16 min bom 24lb/20lb a raid was carried out on the MORTELJE Salient (now 35th Div. front) by 15th Welsh. The raid and preliminary bombardments were supported by Centre group Batteries, and the operation was very successful.	
	30th/1st May	At 1 a.m. in the following night a raid was carried out by 13th [...] brokn on Cliff, Centre group Batteries supported it. Working parties have now heavily engaged in preparing new Gun positions (CuhN3 camouflage).	
			New batteries have taken a certain amount of hostile shelling of batteries: B/121's O.P. (South?) position in B15b has been shelled: C/121 and D/121 have had their [...]. In the Assistance Training "School" close was held 'D' Group Tuf officer and men formed in the "Trench Form" (Sir-hour form) Completion in the Boxing (O.R.) G - 2 to 3 contest.	

G.P. MacLellan
Lieut-Col. Cmdg.
RFA
121 Bde RFA

Army Form C. 2118

WAR DIARY
or
INTELLIGENCE SUMMARY

C/1M April 1917.

(Erase heading not required.)

Place	Date	Hour	Summary of Events and Information	Remarks and references to Appendices
	5th		Still in action on outskirts of Ypres	S.1
	13th		2/Lt C.H. MOORE returned from 2nd Army Artillery School.	S.1
			2/Lt J.H. RIMMER went to " " " " "	S.1
	4th		Battery was shelled. Br-Branch slightly wounded.	S.1
	29th		2/Lt T. THOMPSON promoted Lieutenant. Con-shortag. Occupy pl-	S.1
	30th		Appointed Adjt by Major D.C. Stephenson and 13th with Con-shortag. Occupy pl-	S.1
			Captain W.A.C. Stone	
			Lieutenant J. Thompson	
			2/Lieut. J.H. Rimmer	
			" " C.H. Moore	
			" " C.W. Fitzherbert (went to D/M)	
			" " R.S. Liveing	
			" " J. Arthur	

1961. B.S.M.

R.V. Seymour
Capt. & Major RA
Comd. C/171.

WAR DIARY
or
INTELLIGENCE SUMMARY.

Army Form C. 2118.

A/1 D.R.F.A.

Place	Date	Hour	Summary of Events and Information	Remarks and references to Appendices
1915 April	1st–11th		The battery is still in action between ELVERDINGHE & BRIELEN BELGIUM, at DOWSON'S CORNER. Between the 1st and 11th instants Registration was carried on, and a very few wounds were fired for sniping.	
	19th		On the 19th inst, 150 rds were expended as covering fire for a T.M shoot on the enemies wire from FLASH COT S.round the KRUPP SALIENT.	
	23rd		Capt. Yryyan took temporary command of the battery while Maj. O.d. was at VIII Corp Rest Station Monchoust. On the 23rd inst 150 rds were fired to cover a shoot by the medium T.M's on the enemies wire from FLASH COT to KRUPP SALIENT.	
	29/30		On the night of the 25th/26th. 310 rds were fired on S.O.S. lines between 10 to 10.30 p.m. Result- enemies raid, if attempted, failed. On the night of the 29th/30th. 420 rds were fired on	

WAR DIARY or INTELLIGENCE SUMMARY

Army Form C. 2118.

The enemy front line & support trenches between FLATSH COT and KRUPP SALIENT - time 9.30 p.m. to 9.50 p.m.
At 12.30 am a raid on the MORTELDJE SALIENT was made by the 15th WELSH REGIMENT. The battery fired on the Southern face of KRUPP SALIENT and communication trenches behind. - By 80 rds fired Russet - 1 M.G. Captured, 1 M.G. destroyed and 8 prisoners taken on the 35th Major Townsend assumed command of the Battery.

C.M.G. 9/12/1917

Army Form C. 2118.

Vol /17
121st Bde RFA May 1917

WAR DIARY
or
INTELLIGENCE SUMMARY
(Erase heading not required.)

Reference – Sheet 28.

Place	Date	Hour	Summary of Events and Information	Remarks and references to Appendices
TROIS-TOURS CHATEAU. ARLEUX.	May 1st 1917		Lieut Col. S.P. Rose-Millar D.S.O. commanding. Guile Group 28th DA. at Trois Tours. See last Diary. B/121 D/119 (4 guns) in the Group.	
	4/5 5/6		122 Bde. RFA. took gun positions. Right Group with 6 batteries. A B C and D/121. B/119 and D/115 6 guns – B12 d ½.9 to C14 b 4.2. The Enemy heavily [illegible] shelled Back areas including Plougastel Chateau and Poperinghe during the nights 4/5 and 5/6 hrs, on [illegible] That the whole 4th Army Front retaliated with very heavy bursts of fire. A Trench Trouble Rack Battery 5 minutes, and 11.0 p.m. Firing died down. Repeat this afternoon and 8:45 p.m.	By 4th Army O.O. No.1
	7			
	14/15.		On this night a dummy Raid was carried out in support of a raid on CANADIAN TRENCH by 38th Div. During this night the Enemy attempted 2 raids in which he secured 3 prisoners; one near EATING trench, which was cleared off. One German but captured.	R.S. 33.
	21/22.		During this time in one Battery 115th higher by [Battery] HQ (BSgt Price-Davies) on night 21/22 May, 122 Bde HQ. GSR are from 115 to 7 Bde HQ. is 15 L/t Front 20.16 DA. at Ploegsteert Chateau. 115 Bde. A.F.A. Bri. were ever of L/t bani. Right Bde was taken over by 122 Bde H.Q. 6/1 Front – A/122, B/122 and D/121. There are 2 batteries and 1 section in the C/122 remain in Right Group.	Observer's note near EATING trench, Appendix.
EVERD-INGHE.				

WAR DIARY or INTELLIGENCE SUMMARY

Army Form C. 2118.

Place	Date	Hour	Summary of Events and Information	Remarks and references to Appendices
ELVERDINGHE.	May 1917.			
			During the last 10 days of the month, there has been shooting, harassing fire & gas shoots of the Group, and by the French Artillery on the BOESINGHE SECTOR which we cover. Enemy Trenches have been systematically destroyed as shown in position & counter attack. Special attention has been paid to the S.E. and S.W. of BARBOSA Support, and BARBOSA LANE, (B bk); CARIBOO AVENUE, and trenches in C, I, C and A, d. Harassing fire has also been employed at night on tracks seen and suspected and junctions of trenches bombarded during the day.	
	31st		B/m and C/m 1/D/101 took part in the Practice Barrage on 4.30 p.m. Both bois assisted also in the "Standing Barrage"; the Artillery Barrage being "active"; consisted of Batteries of Rifle Group. Heavy Tr.M.s and Howitzers at the same time bombarded CANAL AVENUE and line in front Nr. (C 7 a) carried out Nr, at 212, Eplice point). Forward positions of bois have certainly suffered damage, but Mr. Taylor, on 188 RFA.	

G. MacGillivray. RFA
comd. 17185 Bde. RFA

31-5-17.

SECRET.   Operation Order No. 1.
                                                7th May, 1917.

RIGHT GROUP - 38th Divisional Artillery.

1. A bombardment of the back areas on the whole 2nd Army Front is being carried out tonight as follows :-

   For 5 minutes from 8.45 p.m. to 8.50 p.m.;
   and again (if ordered) from 11 p.m. to 11.5 p.m.

2. Tasks for RIGHT GROUP, 38th Divisional Artillery are shown in attached table.

3. Rates of fire :-

   18 pdrs. 5 rounds per gun per minute, Half Time Shrapnel, Half H.E.

   4-5" Hows. 4 rounds per gun per minute.

4. If repetition at 11 p.m. is required, the Code word "CHEESE" will be sent.

5. A C K N O W L E D G E.

                                        [signed]
                                        Lieut. Colonel R.F.A.
                                     Commanding RIGHT GROUP R.F.A.

Copy No. 1. O.C. B/119.
         2.   D/119.
         3.   A/121.
         4.   B/121.
         5.   C/121.
         6.   D/121.
         7.   113th Infantry Brigade (for information)
         8.   Diary.
         9.   File.

By ack 7.45 pm.

SECRET.   APPENDIX to Operation Order No. 1.

RIGHT GROUP - 38th Divisional Artillery.

Tasks allotted are as follows :-

18 pdrs.

B/119.   2 Guns.   C.10.c.00.55. :- C.10.c.3.8.   C.T.
         2 guns.   C.9.d.00.25. :- C.9.d.3.8.   C.T.
    Enfilade Section.
         2 guns.   C.8.a.20.95. :- C.2.c.25.20.   C.T.

A/121.   3 guns.   C.9.c.5.5. :- C.9.b.5.1.   Tram line.
         2 guns.   C.9.c.4.8. :- C.9.a.70.15.   C.T.

B/121.   3 guns.   C.1.d.0.3. :- C.1.d.55.72.   C.T.
    (ELVERDINGHE)
         2 guns.   C.8.a.60.27. :- C.8.a.6.6.   Trench & Tram line.

C/121.   2 guns.   C.8.b.8.6. :- Station C.3.a.0.0. Tram line.
         4 guns.   C.8.a.6.6. :- C.2.c.8.2.   Trench & Tram line.

4.5" Hows.

D/119.   1 How.   C.9.a.65.20.
         1 ,,   C.3.c.0.0.   Station.

D/121.(BRIELEN)
         1 How.   C.10.c.5.7.
         1 How.   C.9.d.17.75. Dump.

D/121.   1 How.   C.2.c.8.2.
         1 ,,   C.2.c.25.20.
         1 ,,   C.1.d.10.37.

SECRET.

No. 33

1. A minor Operation will be carried out tonight by 39th Division.

2. A dummy Raid bombardment will be opened on the VON KLUCK front by RIGHT GROUP, 38th D.A. as follows :- — HIGH COMMAND

18 pdrs.

Zero 0.05. A/121. 6 guns front line C.14.b.40.15. — C.15.a.00.10.
C/121. 6 guns front line C.15.a.00.10. — C.15.a.50.15.

0.05 to 0.07. All guns move North by 50 yards every minute to line as follows :-

0.07 till Order "CEASE FIRE"
A/121. C.14.b.82.43. — C.15.a.20.40.
C/121. C.15.a.20.40. — C.15.a.55.41.

4.5" Hows.

Zero till order "CEASE FIRE"
D/121. (BRIELEN Section) 2 Hows. Trench Junctions C.15.a. Central.
D/121. 1 How. C.14.b.7.9.
1 How. C.9.d.0.1.

3. Order to Cease fire will be given from Group.

4. RATES OF FIRE :-
18 pdrs. Zero to 0.05. 4 rounds per gun per minute. ⎫ ½ Shrapnel
0.05 to 0.07. 2 ,, ,, ,, ⎬ ½ HE.
0.07 onwards. 1 ,, ,, ,, ⎭

4.5" Hows. Zero onwards 1 round per How. per minute.

5. Watches will be synchronized at Right Group Headquarters at 8 p.m. today 14th. Each Battery taking part should send a representative with a watch.

6. ACKNOWLEDGE.

Lieut. Colonel R.F.A.

14-5-17. Commanding RIGHT GROUP — 38th D.A.

Copies.
No 1. RA. 39th Div.
2 Left Group. 39th DA.
3 A/121
4 C/121
5 D/121
6 D/119.
7 File.

SECRET.   Operation Order No. 1.
                                                 Copy No. 9

                   LEFT   GROUP – 38th D.A.
----

(1) The Heavy T.M. is bombarding the Enemy's front trench at about
    B.12.b.8.2. commencing at about 2 p.m. today.

(2) B/121. will provide covering fire as under viz :-
            On CARIBOO AVENUE
                C.:.c.4.4. – 3½.5. – 5½.6. – 6.6.
            CANAL DRIVE
            CANAL AVENUE

(3) The 2" T.M's. will bombard enemy's front and support trenches
    between B.12.b.8½.0. and B.12.b.5.5. All available Mortars
    which we can bear on this front will be in action.

(4) Ammunition allotment :-
            18 pdrs. – 100 Shrapnel.
              ,,   – 100 H.E.
            2" T.M's.– Up to 200 rounds.

(5) The signal to open fire will be the opening of fire by the Heavy
    T.M.; on conclusion of Heavy T.M. bombardment the code message
    "FLYING PIG" will be sent, on receipt of which 18 pdrs. and 2"
    T.M's. will cease firing. The Operation may be expected to
    last about 2 hours.

(6) The Infantry are clearing trenches from BRIDGE STREET to the
    Right of the Left Brigade Sector.

(7) ACKNOWLEDGE.

                                        Lieut. Colonel R.F.A.
24-5-17.   Commanding LEFT GROUP 38th D.A.

Copy No. 1.   38th Div. R.A.
      2.   115th Inf. Bde.
      3.   A/121.
      4.   B/121.
      5.   D/121.
      6.   T.M's Left Group.
      7.   RIGHT GROUP R.A.
      8.   File.
      9.   War Diary. ✓

SECRET.   COPY No. 10

LEFT   GROUP :- 38th D.A.   Operation Order No. 3.
==

1. The 2" T.M's. will bombard the area B.6.c.80.98. - d.15.95. -
   05.78. - c.90.87. - 85.80. tomorrow, 28th May, beginning at
   3.15 p.m.
   Up to 150 rounds may be used

2. Covering fire will be as under :-
   D/121.   1 How. MILL.   B.6.d.32.57.
            1 How.   C.1.a.30.30. - 35.25.
   Ammunition :- 50 rounds.

   A/121. Search BABOON SUPPORT.
   Ammunition - 200 rounds.

   B/121. Search CARIBOO AVENUE.
                  BABOON AVENUE.
   Ammunition :- 100 rounds.

3. The shoot may be expected to last about 1½ hours. The signal for
   opening fire will be the opening of the 2" T.M's. At the
   conclusion of the shoot the Code word "FOOTBALL" will be sent to
   Group Headquarters by Officer i/c 2" T.M's

4. ACKNOWLEDGE.

                                                              2/Lt. R.F.A.
27-5-17.   Adjutant LEFT GROUP   38th D.A.

Copy No. 1.   R.A.H.Q. 38th Div.
       2.   O.C. 115th Inf. Bde.
       3.   Right Group 38th D.A.
       4.   A/121.
       5.   B/121.
       6.   D/121.
       7.   Left Group Medium T.M's.
       8.   D.T.M.O.
       9.   War Diary.
      10.   File.

SECRET.   COPY No. 10

LEFT   GROUP - 38th D.A. Operation Order No.5.
_____

1. The 2" T.M.'s. will bombard the Trench MILL - B.6.d.43.60. -
   53.47. - 65.50 and BABOO LANE between the MILL and B.6.d.13.25.
   tomorrow 30th inst, commencing at 1.30 p.m.

2. Covering fire will be as under.-
   A/121. Search BABOON SUPPORT B.6.a.65.72. to the MILL paying
           particular attention to the point B.6.d.07.80.
   B/121. Search CARIBOO AVENUE between B.6.d.65.50. and C.1.a.37.22
   D/121. 1 How. C.1.c.83.72.
           1 How. C.1.c.75.85.
           and trench between these points.

3. Ammunition allotment : 2" T.M's up to 200 rounds.
                           18 pdr batteries, 150 rounds each, half H.E.
                           4.5" Hows. - 50 rounds.

4. Batteries will keep in communication with Left Group T.M. Headquarters (EC.6.) The signal for them to open fire will be
   the commencement of the T.M. Bombardment.
   Operations may be expected to last about 2 hours.

5. The Code word "NAPOO" will be sent to Group Headquarters by O.C.
   Left Group T.M's. on conclusion of Bombardment.

6. A C K N O W L E D G E.

                                           Lieut. Colonel R.F.A.
29-5-17.   Commanding Left Group - 38th D.A.

Copy No.1. H.Q. R.A. 38th D.A.
       2.   H.Q. 115th Infantry Brigade.
       3.   A/121.
       4.   B/121.
       5.   D/121. (Section)
       6.   H.Q. Belgian Artillery.
       7.   O.C. Left M.T.M. Group.
       8.   D.T.M.O.
       9.   File.
      10.   Diary.

SECRET.   E.G. 28.

1. Harrassing fire will be employed at times and places as under:-

May 29th   5.p.m. to 8.p.m.
B/121   50 rounds U.25.a.45.25.-,T.10.00.-.-,T.30.b.85.35.-,
                      25.a.28.50.
D/121   25 rounds, 1 How. U.25.a.45.25
                      1 how. T.30.d.75.90.

Night May 29/30th 9.p.m. to 5.a.m.
A/121   40 rounds) Targets as for
B/121   85   "   ) last night (vide
D/121   25   "   ) E.G.25)

May 30th 6.a.m. to 9.a.m.
B/121   50 rounds E.6.b.9.8.-,C.14.d.10.75.-,U.25.c.
D/121   25 rounds 1 How. C.J.c.75.90.
                      1 how. C.I.c.85.70.

2. ACKNOWLEDGE.

                                           [signature]
                                                    2/Lieutenant R.F.A.
29-5-1917.   Adjutant LEFT GROUP, 38th D.A.

WAR DIARY or INTELLIGENCE SUMMARY

Army Form C. 2118

9/121 (Rt & Centre Secs)
Period 1 to 15/5/17
          16 to 31/5/17.

Place	Date	Hour	Summary of Events and Information	Remarks and references to Appendices
Field	1/5/17	6pm	Fired 28 Rounds at large concrete dug out in Trench at C.14.6.7½. Dugouts laid bare by recent bombardment. Shooting very accurate but heavier shells required to penetrate.	
"	"	6.40pm	Fired 4 Rounds at do. 4 Germans seen to run along trench into dugout. 2 direct hits.	
"	3/5/17	2.35pm to 3.30pm	Fired 21 Rounds at GENERAL FARM. C.3.d.4.8. & CHIMNEY Ho. to test firing with Box Respirators. Satisfactory Result.	
"	"	5.55pm	Fired 18 Rds at Dug out (Concrete) C.14.C.2.1½. Front Trench much damaged.	
"	"	7pm	Fired 12 Rounds at C.8.c.3.0 + C.8.c.2.5½. MINNIE SKIPTON. Excellent Result.	
"	4/5/17	6pm & 7pm	Fired 22 Rds. at Front Line. Re Registration of Night work. Satisfactory	

Army Form C. 2118.

WAR DIARY
or
INTELLIGENCE SUMMARY

(Erase heading not required.)

Instructions regarding War Diaries and Intelligence Summaries are contained in F. S. Regs., Part II. and the Staff Manual respectively. Title Pages will be prepared in manuscript.

Place	Date	Hour	Summary of Events and Information	Remarks and references to Appendices
Field	6/5/17	8.10 A.M.	Fired 5 Rounds at C.14.a.65.70. Working party seen. Party dispersed.	
"	7/5/17	7.30pm	Fired 16 Rounds at large working party. 30 men - in CAESAR'S RESERVE at C.14.c.68.48. Shells fell all among them.	
"	"	10pm	Fired 6 Rds at C.14.a.78.68. To disperse party of work had been continued.	
"	23/5/17	1.5pm	Fired 9 Rounds at C14.b.07. Order from R.G. Excellent detonations.	
"	"	3.30pm	Fired 20 Rounds at BOCHCASTEL EST. Calibration (Shek) Satisfactory.	
"	"	4.15pm	Fired 19 Rounds. KULTUR FARM Calibration 4th Ch. & rounds Siege Artillery. Satisfactory.	
"	"	4.45pm	Fired 20 Rounds at CHEMIN X Road Est. Registration. Much damage to CAESAR. RESERVE.	
"	24/5/17	1.10pm	Fired 100 Rounds at CANDLE TRENCH C.2.C. Retaliation. Excellent.	
"	"	5.25pm	Fired 5 Rounds at KOLN FARM Registration for R.G.3rd Satisfactory	
"	"	3.30pm	Fired 100 Rounds at MAUSER COT C.14.a.37.68. + C.8.C.8.2. R.G.3A. Very accurate. No hostile T.M.s opened till 3.45 pm.	

WAR DIARY or INTELLIGENCE SUMMARY

Army Form C. 2118.

Place	Date	Hour	Summary of Events and Information	Remarks and references to Appendices
Field	25/5/17	5 p.m.	Fired 24 Rds at RICKEM MILL. Calibration of New Gun with Ch 5. Batteries. Very accurate gun.	Very accurate Gun.
"	"	6 p.m.	Fired 16 Rds at C.14.a.85.70. Calibration of New Gun with Ch 1/N.C.T.	
"	"	7 p.m.	Fired 4 rounds on ESSEN FARM. Registration for RG 33/1. Successful. MAUSER COT. C.14.a.20.75.	
"	"	"	2 do. " " "	
"	"	"	1 " " "	
"	26/5/17	5.20 p.m.	Fired 43 rounds at CHIMNEY 40. Registration for shoot at 6pm. Successful.	
"	"	6 p.m.	Fired 200 Rounds on TRAMWAY STATION & Sdings. C.20.a.4.4 & district Sector Somme. Very effective shoot. Cross observation from FRASCATI & JOYENCE O.Ps. Large quantities of grain & stores up.	
"	27/5/17	10.15 a.m.	Fired 7 Rounds at C.20.8½.3½. To test ZERO. Results Good.	
"	"	12.30 p.m.	" 36 Rounds on C.14.6.03.03. C.14.c.74.95. C.18.a.28.72. C.13.6.89.72. Registration of Night lines. Successful.	
"	"	1.30 p.m.	Fired on MINNIE SKIPTON. Effective.	

Army Form C. 2118.

WAR DIARY
or
INTELLIGENCE SUMMARY

(Erase heading not required.)

Instructions regarding War Diaries and Intelligence Summaries are contained in F. S. Regs., Part II. and the Staff Manual respectively. Title Pages will be prepared in manuscript.

Place	Date	Hour	Summary of Events and Information	Remarks and references to Appendices
Field	27.5.17	11 pm	Fired 20 Rds on C.3.a.7.6.	
		11.50 pm	C.3.a.25.58.	O.O. No. 2.
	28.5.17	12.25am	C.3.a.23.18.	
	do	1.55am	STRAY FARM.	
	do	2.10AM		
	28.5.17	3.10AM	Fired 148 Rds. on NIGHT LINES. S.O.S Call.	
"	28.5.17	5.30pm	Fired 42 Rounds at IRON CROSS. Registration at divisional rate on houses	
"		6 firing 8 pm	Fired 148 Rounds at TRAMWAY & ROAD JUNCTION C.3.6.4.6. to 4.8.6. to damage same & obstruct traffic into the "INGS". Road for tonights operation. Got very good detonations, several rails seem to be thrown up.	
"	"	10.15pm	Fired 6 Rounds on C.3.d.7.5 to the "INGS" C.4.a. O.O No. 5.	
"	29.5.17	1.22am	Fired 35 Rounds on NIGHT LINES. Orders from Group	
"	"	3.45am	Fired 6 Rounds at C.3.d.7.5 to the "INGS" C.4.a. O.O. No 5.	
"	"	4.15am	6 Rounds	do

Army Form C. 2118.

WAR DIARY
or
INTELLIGENCE SUMMARY

(Erase heading not required.)

Instructions regarding War Diaries and Intelligence Summaries are contained in F. S. Regs., Part II. and the Staff Manual respectively. Title Pages will be prepared in manuscript.

Place	Date	Hour	Summary of Events and Information	Remarks and references to Appendices
Field	29.5.17	10 A.m to 11 A.m	Fired 30 Rds at KOLN FARM. Registration for wire cutting.	
"	"	"	100 Rds at C.14.6. Wire cutting. Detonations were very good. Wire cut through out.	
"	"	12 Noon	Fired 16 Rounds at PILCKEM MILL. Checking Lines.	
"	"	6.30pm to 8.0pm	Fired 50 Rounds at Grde BARRIERE Cross Roads. O. U. successful. CHIMNEY Ho. (TRAMWAY TURNING).	
"	30.5.17	5.30pm	Fired 9 Rounds at GRAND BARRIERE Ho. Group orders.	
"	"	6.30am to 9 A.m	Fired 41 Rds at Cross Roads at GRAND BARRIERE Ho. Rds at PERISCOPE HOUSE & CHIMNEY HOUSE. O.O.	
"	"	10.30 A.m	Fired 24 Rounds at CACTUS RESERVE. Group orders.	
"	"	3 pm	Fired 520 Rounds at CAESAR'S AVENUE. Bombardment the Trench which is nearby enfilade from E.H.41) was thoroughly searched with apparently good effect. Knife rests were thrown up in front of the Trench. The Trench (which here runs from (green) before hit shown is now much advanced. Apparent. Planks were thrown up just North of GALLWITZ FARM.	
"	"	6 pm to 9 pm	Fired 40 Rounds at IRON CROSS. O.O. Accurate.	

Army Form C. 2118.

WAR DIARY
or
INTELLIGENCE SUMMARY

(Erase heading not required.)

Instructions regarding War Diaries and Intelligence Summaries are contained in F. S. Regs., Part II. and the Staff Manual respectively. Title Pages will be prepared in manuscript.

Place	Date	Hour	Summary of Events and Information	Remarks and references to Appendices
Field	3/5/17	5.0 am	Fired 25 Rounds at GALLWITZ FARM. O.O.	
"	"	12.40pm	" 12 " at PILCKEM X Roads Retaliation, accurate	
"	"	3.15pm	" 121 " WELSH FARM. Calibration 4th ch. (N.C.T + B missile) Probable very regular, N.C.T very irregular, several direct hits	
"	"	4.30pm	" 63 " R.G.45. Practice Barrage. As seen from FRASCATI the Barrage seemed highly effective for the last 20 to 25 minutes. After that a large percentage of 15 pdr. shrapnel burst high. The screening effect was negligible, the back area near TELEGRAPH H0. GABLE H0. MOLTKE Redoubt etc. being visible throughout the proceedings.	
"	"	5.45pm	" 60 Rds at House C.10.6.05.15. Possible O.P. 9 direct hits. House badly mauled + probably now unserviceable as an O.P.	
"	"	5.30pm	" 16 Rds at House. C.9.d.9.31. Possible O.P. 3 direct hits, house demolished.	
"	"	5.45pm	" 76 Rds at VON WERDER H0. Suspected Gunpits. 2 direct hits, but ground floor seems to be strongly fortified.	
"	"	7.45pm	" 30 Rds at Railway, C.2.a.43 to C.2.a.75. Smoke of train. Smoke cleared for 2 minutes, but recommenced. Train was probably in a light railway. Further off.	

Army Form C. 2118.

WAR DIARY
or
INTELLIGENCE SUMMARY

(Erase heading not required.)

Place	Date	Hour	Summary of Events and Information	Remarks and references to Appendices
Field	31/5/17	8pm to 9pm	Fired 20 Rounds at IRON CROSS. Harrassing fire accurate	
"		9.15pm	Fired 12 Rounds on MINNIE SKIPTON Group orders. Effective	

31st May 1917.

Major RFA
Comdg D/121 Bde.

Copy No 13

Zero hour was at 1.24 am

ACKNOWLEDGE

WAR DIARY
INTELLIGENCE SUMMARY

121st Bde.8, R.H.A
Antwerp Sheet 20   June 1917

Place	Date	Hour	Summary of Events and Information	Remarks and references to Appendices
ELVERDINGHE CHATEAU	June 1917		Under Lieut Col. G.P. MacClellan, in command of Left Group 30th D.A. Batteries in the Group — A/121, B/121, and 1 section B/121. Position as in last diary. From this Wurting was done during the first 2 weeks of June, chiefly in support of operations South of YPRES Salient. Many shoots were carried out in conjunction with Left Group Heavies. Trench mortars attacked silent shorts. Main shoots harassing fire on supplies on Ridge back behind trou ares up to a/c the operation of June 7th v. Attached Schemes, E.G. 49.	F.G.49.
	3/4 (night)		One section of A/121 was moved into a position at B.10.6.5.5.45 to be prepared to enfilade which we carried our artillery almost daily on km wire in front of CANAL DRIVE and CANAL DRIVE (Lichar C.7a) with KRUPP Salient.	3/130A DO No.65
	3rd June 7th 3.10AM		Group Batteries took part in a Practice Barrage 30th D.A.	DO No.65
			Being the Zero hour for WYTSCHAETE attack and carried out Harrassing Fire during the rest of the combatment in support, day major.	Left Group OO No 6 & (3rd DA) OO
	8/9 (night)		B/101 supported attack by 13th Welsh & C/7d.C.S.z ... Owing to situation No 67 (64) in 16th Corps Front. The wishes barely could not taken cold the through trench the rail was carried out Shortly in the following major	3rd DA OO No 6/7 6/9 On fa Jungs OO No 33

WAR DIARY
INTELLIGENCE SUMMARY.

121 Bde RFA. June 1917.

Army Form C. 2118.

Place	Date	Hour	Summary of Events and Information	Remarks and references to Appendices
WOESTEN	8/9 June (midnight)		The battery position of A/121 at ZIZI (T.20) was heavily bombarded by HE during the night, nearly 1000 rounds being fired. 2nd Lieut A. Fox died of wounds from the enemy's concentration of fire & one Gunner was killed, and Lieut H.W. Turner and four men wounded. The bombardment continued of the enemy's batteries during the next two days nights. The battery was withdrawn, showing great spirit, after this period, only in emergency. The enemy were very active about this time. A/121 were heavily shelled in some cases by higher level shells and also three rounds were fired (as is the forward section position was seen) shells did not the forward section in the section also shelled. The forward section in B/121 was moved to ELVERDINGHE Village, in active during the grade enemy's firstly on ELVERDINGHE and was Railways found the villages. About this date the 115th left Batt. were relieved by 2 Nd Guards Bgde in the BOESINGHE Sector. The 115th CG NW (?) being in the front line on the night 7/8th Our section 1/A/122 came under left group A or B.10.0.1.0.	
	15.			
	17/18/ 18/19		On the nights 17/18 18/19 of June the left group RFA was relieved by 114 Bde RFA (Guards SA). The 121 Bde H.Q. with A/121 & B/121 duly on action 121 were back to the wagon lines.	

WAR DIARY

Army Form C. 2118.

INTELLIGENCE SUMMARY. 121 B.N. R.F.A. June 1917

Place	Date	Hour	Summary of Events and Information	Remarks and references to Appendices
KRUITHOEK	June 3	9.17	The batteries A/B/121 and A/101 were sent to HERZEELE to refit. B/121 had great difficulty getting its animals which showed her in action, in the forward area. Orders received at 1.15pm and 6.0 pm were left behind by A and B/101 to continue the consolidation of the B.R. position of this and on others. C/121 and A/121 are constructing their own positions.	

M.Mmm
Captain R.F.A.
to Major A.T. R.A.
and 121 R.F.R.A

SECRET.

AMENDMENT to ARTILLERY RAID PROGRAMME.

Two Howitzers of D/121. will be at the disposal of the Counter Battery Staff Officer XIth Corps for Counter Battery work from Zero onwards. The targets for D/59. and D/121. will accordingly be re-allotted as follows :-

Zero to + 5'

    D/59.   I.11.c.99.72.
                  I.11.a.80.32.
                         93.61.
                  11.b.00.80.
    D/121.   I.11.d.91.93. *
                  I.11.a.87.21.

+ 5' onwards.

    D/59.   I.11.c.99.72.
                    5.d.58.05.
                    5.d.18.25.
                  11.b.85.99.
    D/121.   I.11.d.91.93. *
                  11.c.82.25.

* A proportion of Gas shell will be used on this target if the wind be favourable. 50% Gas shell will be used by D/121. in their Counter Battery work.

S E C R E T.

LEFT GROUP :- 38th D.A.

Artillery Programme

1. 18 pdrs.

Zero to + 3'

A/59. (2 guns) I.11.a.45.12. ;- 35.22.
       (2 guns) I.11.a.35.22. ;- 40.30.
       (2 guns) I.11.a.40.30. ;- 58.34.

B/121. (5 guns) I.11.a.58.34. ;- 60.54.
       (1 gun)   I.11.b.25.90. ;- 5.d.40.02.

B/59. (6 guns) I.11.a.60.54. ;- 65.78.

C/121. (4 guns) I.11.a.65.78. ;- 70.96.
       (2 guns) I.11.c.98.75. ;- 98.53.

A/121. (6 guns) I.11.a.70.96. ;- 5.c.79.14.

C/59. (2 guns) I.5.c.79.14. ;- 90.22.
       (2 guns) INANE ALLEY I.5.d.40.02. ;- 12.a.10.81.

376 Bty. (6 guns) I.11.a.83.26. ;- 94.55.

377 Bty. (5 guns) I.11.a.94.55. ;- b.03.85.
         (1 gun) I.11.b.03.79. ;- 25.90.

+ 3' to + 5'

A/59. (6 guns) I.11.a.62.14. ;- 58.34.
Remainder.   No change.

+ 5' to + 9'

A/59. (2 guns) I.11.a.75.17. ;- 72.27.
       (4 guns) I.11.a.35.22. ;- 61.15.
B/121. (5 guns) I.11.a.72.27. ;- 74.47.
       (1 gun) I.11.b.25.90. ;- 5.d.40.02. (no change)

B/59. (6 guns) I.11.a.74.47. ;- 79.69.

C/121. (4 guns) I.11.a.79.69. ;- 85.87.
       (2 guns) I.11.c.98.75. ;- 98.53. (no change)

A/121. (6 guns) I.11.a.85.87. ;- 5.c.93.05.

C/59.   }
376 Bty. }   No change.
377 Bty. }

-2-

+9' to +16'

A/59.   (2 guns)   I.11.a.88.08. ; – 86.18.
         (4 guns)   I.11.a.35.22. ; – 61.15. (no change)

B/121. (5 guns)   I.11.a.86.18. ; – 88.36.
         (1 gun)   I.11.b.25.90.; – 5.d.40.02. (no change)

B/59.   (6 guns)   I.11.a.88.36. ; – 92.57.

C/121. (4 guns)   I.11.a.92.57. ; – 98.75.
         (2 guns)   I.11.c.98.75. ; – 98.53. (no change)

A/121. (6 guns)   I.11.a.98.75. ; – b.05.95.

C/59. ⎫
376 Bty. ⎬   No change.
377 Bty. ⎭

+16' to +1 hr.45'

A/59.   (2 guns)   Railway I.11.b.05.11. – 12.c.80.70.
         (4 guns)   I.11.a.35.22. ; – 61.15. (no change)

B/121. (5 guns)   I.11.a.61.15. ; – 73.12.; – 90.05.; – b.10.05.
         (1 gun)   I.11.b.53.44. and I.11.b.53.62.

B/59.   (6 guns)   I.11.b.10.05.; – 35.87. This battery will
                    search and sweep the area bounded by this
                    line, the Railway and INANE ALLEY.

376 Bty. (4 guns) I.11.b.10.05. ; – 18.31.
         (2 guns) I.5.d.40.02. ; – 12.a.10.81.

C/121. (4 guns)   I.11.b.10.05. – 18.31. – 27.53
         (2 guns) INCARNATE AVENUE I.11.c.55.42.; – 17.b.35.75.

377 Bty. (6 guns) I.11.b.27.53. ; – 38.85.

A/121. (6 guns)   I.11.b.38.85. ; – 5.c.98.13.

C/59.   (2 guns)   I.5.c.98.13. ; – 87.20.
         (2 guns) INANE ALLEY I.12.a.10.82. ; – 90.05.

18 pdrs on the creeping barrage will sweep 5' and those on the
back of the Box sufficient to cover the front allotted to
them.   There will be no practice barrage but B.C's
will please collaborate with a view to eliminating
gaps in the barrage.

2.   4-5" Hows.

Zero to +5'

D/121. 1 How.   I.11.d.91.93. ✱
         1 How.   I.11.c.99.72.
         1 How.   I.11.c.65.75.
         1 How.   I.11.a.87.21.

D/59.   1 How.   I.11.a.80.32.
                  I.11.a.93.61.
                  I.11.b.00.80.
                  I.11.b.85.99.

+5' to +1 hr. 45'

  D/121. 1 How. I.11.d.91.93. ✻
        I.11.c.99.72.
        I.11.c.65.75.
        I.11.c.82.25.

  D/59. 1 How. I.5.d.16.25.
        I.5.d.58.05.
        I.11.b.85.99.
        I.5.d.00.32.

✻ If wind is suitable a proportion of Gas shell will be fired on this target.

3. Medium T.M's will take on Hostile T.M's; actual targets will be allotted on Zero day according to which have been most recently active.

4. Heavy Artillery are being asked to do Counter Battery work from Zero onwards.

5. Rates of fire

 Zero to +5' 18 pdrs. 4 rds per gun per minute.
        4-5" Hows. 3 ,, ,, ,,
 +5' to +18' 18 pdrs. 3 ,, ,, ,,
        4-5" Hows. 2 ,, ,, ,,
 +18' to +1 hr 45' 18 pdrs ⎤
        4-5" Hows. ⎦ 1 rd per gun per minute.

This throughout as much as possible.

6. Ammunition 18 pdrs.

 Zero to +9' All T.S. except batteries on Support Line which will use 50% H.E.

 +9' to +16' All T.S.

 +16' onwards. All Batteries 50% T.S., 50% H.E. except those on sides of the box which will fire all T.S.
       A corrector to give 70% grazes to be used until the box is formed at +16' then an effective corrector, except that guns not on the creeping barrage not front trenches will use an effective corrector throughout.

SECRET.   AD.0078.

LEFT GROUP. - 38th D. A.

1. A shoot will take place tomorrow (2nd Dec.) as follows :-

<u>101 S. Bty.</u>   CELT SWITCH.

    1 How.   C.23.b.38.68.
    1 How.   C.23.b.42.82. , - 46.92.
    1 How.   C.17.d.50.06.
    1 How.   C.17.d.53.19. , - 54.31.

<u>6" T.M.</u>   C.23.b.38.70. , - 45.90.

<u>D/121.</u>   CELT DRIVE.

    1 How.   C.23.b.55.84. , - 63.90.
    1 How.   C.23.b.71.92. , - 96.97.
    1 How.   C.23.b.96.97. , - C.18.c.18.04.

<u>C/121.</u>   Enfilade CELT DRIVE.

    C.23.b.42.80. , - C.18.c.80.24.

<u>B/121.</u>   C.23.b.18.22. , - 37.67.

<u>A/121.</u>   3 guns   LESCURSINS FME.

    3 guns.   C.24.a.60.29. , - 90.10.

<u>97th Bty.</u>   C.17.d.17.43. , - 40.62. , - 52.34. , - 22.19.

2. <u>Time</u> - 2 p.m. - 3 p.m.

3. <u>Ammunition.</u> 6" Hows. 200 rounds.

    6" T.M.   100   ,,
    4-5" Hows. 40 rounds a gun.
    18 pdrs.   20   ,,   ,,

18 pdrs. will fire in short bursts using ½ Shrapnel and
½ H.E. (delay)

A/121. will open fire 5 minutes after commencement of
shoot to catch "Spectators".

4. ACKNOWLEDGE BY WIRE.

                                Major R.F.A.
1:12:17.   Commanding Left Group. - 38th D.A.

Copies to Group Batteries

SECRET.   AD.0080.

LEFT GROUP 38th D.A.

1. A combined shoot will take place ~~tomorrow 6th~~ on Saturday 8th Dec. as under :

   6" Hows.   INCENSE AVENUE
                 I.17.a.40.54. – 83.10.

   4-5" Hows.   I.17.d.01.82. to ~~&~~ I17d 60.75
                 ~~& I.17.a.26.07.~~

   9.45" T.M.   I.17.a.40.54. – 30.60.

   6" T.M. (CENTRAL)   I.17.a.55.74. – 40.77.

   6" T.M. (BRICK ST.) I.17.a.23.36.

   18 pdrs. A/121. ~~3 guns enfilade tram line I.17.a.55.74. to~~
                    ~~I.17.b.75.10.~~
                    ~~3 guns enfilade trench I.17.d.93.67. to~~
                    ~~I.18.c.30.20.~~

            B/121. ~~I.17.d.0.8. – 93.67.~~
            C/121. ~~I.17.a.23.36. – 60.38. – I.17.d.0.8.~~
            97th Bty. ~~I.11.c.80.22. – I.17.b.62.32.~~

2. Time – ~~11 a.m. to 12 noon.~~
          1 pm – 2 pm

3. Ammunition. 6" Hows. – 200 rounds.
                4-5" Hows. – 100 ,,
                9.45" T.M. – 25   ,,
                6" T.M's. – 200   ,,
                18 pdrs. – 10 rds per gun (Shrapnel) in bursts.

4. ACKNOWLEDGE BY WIRE.

                                              [signature] Capt. R.F.A.
   5:12:17.   Adjutant Left Group 38th D.A.

X 18 pdrs. All guns which can bear will fire two of them bursts of shrapnel during first 15 minutes of shoot, along INCENSE AVENUE from front line to I 17 d 00.82

S E C R E T.

RIGHT GROUP 38TH. D.A.

OPERATION ORDER No. 33.

Left Group

Two minor operations will take place to-night with the object of securing identification.

1.)
A.) By 10th. Welsh Regt. party under 2/Lieut. HUGHES.
    Point of entry - KRUPP SALIENT C.14.a.8.0.

B.) By 15th. Welsh Regiment. party under 2/Lieut. STEPHENS.
    Point of entry - C.7.d.10.85.

ZERO HOUR in both cases will be at 11.30.p.m.

Artillery action will be in both cases consist of a two minutes intense bombardment at the point of entry and on enemy fire trench in vicinity, followed by a Pocket Barrage which will continue for 15 minutes, all fire ceasing, unless otherwise ordered by Group H.Q. at ZERO plus 17'

2.(A) ARTILLERY ACTION IN SUPPORT OF 10TH. WELSH
      OPERATION AT C.14.a.8.0.

The party will consist of 1 Officer and about 18 other Ranks in 3 small parties.
      Assembly position C.14.c.7.8. - C.14.c.8.8.

At 11.30.p.m. (ZERO TIME) Guns will open an intense bombardment follows:-

      11.30.p.m. to 11.32.p.m.

"A"/122. 6 Guns. - Enfilade enemy trench from C.14.a.72.00. to
                   C.14.b.20.05.
                   These Guns will fire on enemy trench line
                   and just in front of it in NO MAN'S LAND
                   during these two minutes.
   Ammunition - Time shrapnel giving 50% grazes.

"C"/121. 2 Guns. - Enemy front line C.14.a.72.00. to
(BANAGHER).   C.14.a.6.1.
"C"/121. 4 Guns. - Enemy front line C.14.a.6.1.to C.14.a.3.4.
(BARROW)
   Ammunition - Ammunition ½ H.E. & ½ T.S. giving 70% grazes

"B"/122. 2 Guns. - Enfilade CALABASH AVENUE from C.14.b.04.21.
- (Pittsburg)   to C.14.b.2.5.
   Ammunition. - Time shrapnel giving 70% grazes.

Rates of fire for the above 18-Pdrs will be -
      5 rounds per gun per minute during this period.

"D"/121. 4 Hows. - 1 How. - KOLN FARM.
(YPRES)   1 How. - C.14.b. 1. 1.
                    1 "   - C.14.b. 2. 5.
                    1 "   - C.14.b.75.17.

"D"/122. 2 Hows. - 1 "   - FLASH COT.
(SKIBEEN)   1 "   - C.14.a.20.55.

      11.32.p.m. to 11.47.p.m.

At 11.32.p.m.
18-Pdrs. "A"/122.6 Guns. - Will switch to the left and enfilade
                           from C.14.a.60.25. to C.14.b.2.5.

"C"/121. 2 Guns. - Will lift and enfilade OAKS WALK from
(BANAGHER)   C.14.a.7.4. to C.14.a.9.6.

/Contd.

O.O.33. Sheet 2.

At 11.32.a.m.

18-Pdrs.
The remaining Guns of "C"/121)
and section of Guns "B"/122.) Will continue on same objectives.

Rate of fire. for 18-Pdrs during this period will be :-
3 rounds per Gun per minute.

Ammunition. As in previous period.

4.5" Hows.
Objectives of all 4.5" Hows. will remain the same as in previous period, with the exception that No.2. How "D"/121 will switch to the right from C.14.b.1.1. to C.14.b.2.1.

Rate of fire.for 4.5" Hows. during this period :-
2 rounds per How per minute.

All fire will cease at 11.47.p.m.

Medium T.M's.
One medium T.M will open fire from C.13.b.3.4. as soon as Batteries open at 11.30.p.m. firing on CAESAR'S NOSE. Ceasing fire at 11.47.p.m.

COMMUNICATIONS.
An Officer of the 10th. Welsh will be at POST 19 (C.14.c.6.8) in communication by Power Buzzer with O.C.,10th.Welsh at LANCASHIRE FARM. The latter will be in communication with Maj. Stephenson DSO. MC. at O.P. CONTOUR 19, thence to Right Group Headquarters.

3.)(B) ARTILLERY ACTION IN SUPPORT OF
13TH.WELSH RAID AT C.7.d.10.63.

The party will consist of 1 Officer and about 12 men.
Assembly position - C.7.d.12.40.

At 11.30 p.m. Guns will open intense fire,as follows :-

11.30.p.m. to 11.32.p.m.

18-Pounders.
"B"/121. 5 Guns.   ) - Enfilade CACTUS TRENCH from C.7.c.50.74.
(Left Group ELVERDINGHE)   to C.7.d.10.65.

"C"/122. 3 Guns.   - Enfilade trench from C.7.d.10.65. to
(B.21.b.4.5.)   C.7.d.40.67.

The flank Guns of the above Batteries must overlap at C.7.d.10.65. (the point of entry) during the above period.

"B"/122. 2. Guns. - From KIEL COT to C.7.d.8.4.
(BRIELEN FARM)

"C"/122. 2 Guns. - From C.7.d.40.67. to C.7.d.5.6.
CANAL BANK.

Rate of fire for all the above 18-Pdrs for this period will be :-
5 rounds per gun per minute.

Ammunition. "B"/121 and 3 Guns "C"/122 at B.21.b.4.5.
Time shrapnel giving 50% grazes.
Remaining Guns "C"/122 and "B"/122.
½ H.E. and ½ T?S.,giving 50% grazes.

/Contd.

-2-

4. RATE OF FIRE.

Bursts at irregular intervals during both periods, under arrangements to be made by Group Commanders and D.T.M.O.

5. AMMUNITION.

18-pdrs. 2/3rds. Shrapnel 1/3rd. H.E.

6. ACKNOWLEDGE.

[signature]

Captain, R.A.
Brigade Major 38th. Divisional Artillery.

Issued at 4·50 p.m.
7th. June 1917.

Copies to:-

R.A. VIII Corps.
38th. Div. "G" (7).
VIII Corps H.A.
Right Group. (8)
Left Group (4)
D.T.M.O.
39th. D.A.
4th. Belgian Artillery.
D.M.G.O.

Copy No. 12

38th. Divisional Artillery Operation Order No. 68.

1. (a) It is possible that a local relief in the 38th. LANDWEHR Regiment will take place on the BOESINGHE Front between 10 and 11 pm. to-night.
   The 38th. Divisional Artillery will co-operate with 115th. Infantry Brigade, VIII Corps H.A. and 115th. M.G. Coy. in interfering with the relief.

   (b) In addition to this, the Gas Projectors and Smoke Candles which were to have been let off last night, had the wind been favourable, will be let off to-night if the wind remains favourable.

   The action of the 38th. D.A. in support of this operation will be as detailed in para. 3 (b) 38th. Divisional Artillery Operation Order No. 67, except that the bursts of fire will be carried out between Zero plus 30 and Zero plus 60, instead of between Zero plus 20 and Zero plus 50.

   If there is a dead calm, Gas Projectors will be let off: but the smoke Candles will not be let off, unless there is a wind blowing towards the enemy's lines.

   Code word for "Gas will be let off but not smoke" ... BRIELEN.

   Zero hour for Gas and Smoke will be (11 p.m.)

2. With regard to para. 1.(a) the following are the arrangements :—

   (a) VIII Corps H.A. has been asked to shell the detraining point (LANCIER Fm.- U.13.d.1.5.)

   (b) 115th. M.G. Coy. will fire on CANAL DRIVE, YPRES-THOROUT Railway, and open spaces between ARTILLERY WOOD and WOOD 14 and 15.

   (c) Rifle Grenade and Stokes Mortar Fire on BABOON TRENCH.

3. Action of 38th. Divisional Artillery will be as follows :—

   10 p.m. to 11 p.m. and 12.15 a.m. to 1 a.m.

   18-pdrs. Enfilade Section "B"/122 and 1 Section "B"/121 — CARIBOO TRENCH between CARIBOO AVENUE and BABOO DRIVE.

   "A"/121 — BABOON SUPPORT in neighbourhood of MILL.

   2 Sections "B"/121 — CANAL DRIVE.

   4.5" Hows.— "D"/122 (unless employed on counter-battery work) — CANAL DRIVE.

   1 Section "D"/121 (ELVERDINGHE) Trench Junctions at C.1.a.18.72 and C.1.a.38.24.

   2" T.M's. (1) Area about B.12.b.9.8.
   (2) Area about B.6.d.1.8.

   Heavy T.M. CANAL DRIVE keeping as far N. as possible.

   4/

- 2 -

G.O.C., 114th Infantry Brigade, after consultation with O.C. "Q" Coy. Special Brigade R.E., will decide as to whether Smoke and Projectors will be used, notifying units concerned in the following code :-

Projectors and smoke will be discharged .... m "POPERINGHE ...m"

Discharge of Projectors and Smoke postponed . "WATOU".

4. AMMUNITION.

  Zero to Zero plus 20. 50% of all 18-pdrs. will employ smoke shell: remainder Shrapnel.

  Zero plus 20 onwards. 2/3rds. Shrapnel, 1/3rd. H.E.

5. RATES OF FIRE.

  Zero to Zero plus 2. - 18-pdrs. 5 rounds per gun per minute.
         4.5" Hows. 2 " " how. " "

  Zero plus 2 to Zero plus 10.
       18-pdrs. 3 rounds per gun per minute.
       4.5" Hows. 1 round per how. per minute.

  Zero plus 10 to Zero plus 20.
       18-pdrs. 2 rounds per gun per minute.
       4.5" Hows. 1 round per how. per minute.

  Zero plus 20 onwards. Bursts of fire, as ordered by Group Commanders.

6. Group Commanders will detail special Officers to note all action taken by the enemy, with a view to turning it to advantage in subsequent operations. Apart from reporting important events immediately, half hourly reports will be furnished to R.A.H.Q. by Groups from Zero to Zero plus 3 hours.

7. Zero hour and arrangements for synchronising watches will be notified later.

8. ACKNOWLEDGE.

Issued at 5.15 p.m.
6th June 1917.

              Captain, R.A.
         Brigade Major 38th Divisional Artillery.

Copies to :-

R.A. VIII Corps.
38th Div. "G". (7)
VIII Corps H.A.
Right Group (8)
Left Group (4)
D.T.M.O.
39th D.A.
4th Belgian Arty.
D.M.G.O.

SECRET.

Copy No. 19

38th. Divisional Artillery Operation Order No. 67.

1. The 38th. Division will make a demonstration with Artillery and Machine Guns on the night 6/7th. June or early in the morning on the 7th.

   If the wind is favourable Smoke Bombs, Candles and Gas Projectors will be used as follows :-

   Smoke :- Along the front from C.14.5. to C.7.4. (inclusive).

   Gas Projectors on CADDIE RESERVE, CAESAR RESERVE and CHEMIN TRENCH.

2. R.A., 38th. Division No.G.S.2201 is cancelled.

   Action of 38th. Divisional Artillery will be as follows :-

   Zero to Zero plus 20.
   18-pdrs. - 2 batteries Right Group will barrage the Salients in the reserve line at about C.15.a.4.5., C.14.b.9.4., and C.14.b.3.4.
   2 batteries Right Group and 2 batteries Left Group will barrage the line CANDLE TRENCH, C.2.d.1.0. - PILCKEM MILL - CANCER TRENCH - TELEGRAPH Ho. the dividing line between Groups being SAPEUR Ho.

   At Zero plus 20 "C"/121 will come under the orders of the Counter-battery Staff Officer.

   4.5" Hows. Right (2 Hows. search CALABASH LANE.
              Group (4 Hows.   HINDENBURG FARM.

              Left Group   2 Hows. search trench between TELEGRAPH Ho. and LIEVRE CABARET.

   From Zero onwards "D"/122 (4 Hows.) will be at the disposal of the Counter - battery Staff Officer for neutralizing work.

   T.M's. - All available heavy and medium T.M's will barrage the front and support lines from C.14.a.8.0. to KIEL COT.

3. (a) If the wind is unfavourable for the discharge of Gas Projectors, all guns and Hows., with the exception of those allotted for Counter-battery work, will be employed on harassing fire on roads and communications under arrangements to be made by Group Commanders from Zero plus 20 onwards throughout the day.

   (b) If the wind is favourable the following will be the action taken :-

   Zero plus 20 to Zero plus 50.
   18-pdrs. - 3 batteries Right Group and "B"/121 will fire bursts on the three communication trenches leading South from PILCKEM: fire will not be directed South of a line drawn East and West through GALIWITZ FARM.
   The area in between the above three trenches will be thoroughly searched: there should be six bursts, each of about 4 rounds gun fire.
   "A"/121 will fire similar bursts on CACTUS RESERVE from CACTUS JUNCTION to C.7.b.92.12.

   4.5" Hows. - (less 4 Hows. "D"/122) will bombard the area PILCKEM MILL - CANCER TRENCH - LIEVRE CABARET - PILCKEM CROSS ROADS.

   Zero plus 50 onwards :-
   All guns and Hows., less those doing counter-battery work, will carry out harassing fire as in (a) above.

SECRET.   COPY No. 5

        LEFT   GROUP   38th D.A. Operation Order No. 6
....

            38th Divl. Artillery O.O. No. 67 & attached.

(1) Reference Para 2.
    A/121. will barrage trench between TELEGRAPH HO. and Trench
    Junction C.2.c.07.60.
    B/121. from C.2.c.07.60. to SAPEUR HO.

(2) Reference Para 3 (b)
    B/121. will fire on Communication trench running South from
    SAPEUR HO.
    Reference Para 3. (a)
    Orders as to harassing fire will be issued from Group.
    Should communications break down, 40 rounds per hour will be
    fired by 18 pdr. batteries on points already allotted for
    harassing fire.
    The forward Section A/121. will fire harassing fire on
    WIJDENDRIFT and its approaches, U.21.a.

(3) Reference Para 6.   Both O.P's must be manned by an Officer
    by half an hour before Zero Hour, who will report all important
    events to Group Headquarters as they occur, and will also
    send brief half hourly reports to the Adjutant by 'phone.

(4) A C K N O W L E D G E.

                                            2/Lt. R.F.A.
6-6-17.   Adjutant LEFT GROUP 38th D.A.

Copy No. 1.   A/121.
       2.   B/121.
       3.   D/121. (Section)
       4.   Diary.
       5.   File.

S E C R E T.

EG.54.

(1) At 4.30 p.m. tomorrow (June 5th) 2" T.M's. will bombard
BABOON SUPPORT from B.6.a.50.30. - 85.00.
Up to 200 rounds may be used. (Cancelled)

(2) A/121. will cut wire in front of CANAL DRIVE as today.
400 rounds, starting 4.30 p.m. (Cancelled)

4 Guns - BaBoon Suppt
C.6 Wounds (H.E. Sch. i.) } 400 rds.

(3) B/121. Search trench C.1.d.57.70. - C.2.a.30.15. - 300 rounds   400

(4) D/121. will engage suspected O.P's on S.W. edge of WOOD 15.
150

(5) A C K N O W L E D G E.

[signature]
2/Lt. R.F.A
Adjutant Left Group R.F.A.

4-6-17.

S E C R E T.   EG 49

HARASSING FIRE

Scheme 1.   A/121.   C.1.a.40.00. - c.70.90 - 92.47.
            B/121.   Search Tramway C.2.a.22.30. - U.27.c.80.45.
            D/121.   U.27.c.25.57.
                     U.27.c.10.80.

Scheme 2.   A/121.   Search ARTILLERY WOOD.
            B/121.   MILITARY ROAD in U.27.c. and a.
            D/121.   C.1.c.75.90.
                     C.1.c.85.70.

Scheme 3.   A/121.   Search CANCER TRENCH from C.1.d.87.70. to SAPPER HO.
            B/121.   MILITARY ROAD in U.25.c., d., and b.
                     Tramway U.25.d.3.4.   - b.85.50.
            D/121.   Tramway Sidings about C.2.a.40.35.

Scheme 4.   A/121.   Trenches about C.1.c. Central.
            B/121.   Road U.25.a.45.25. - d.12.50.
            D/121.   U.25.a.45.25.

Scheme 5.   B/121.   Tramway U.25.c.27.45. - d.12.50.
            D/121.   Dugouts etc about U.27.c.30.50.

                                              G.P. MacClellan
                                              Lieut. Colonel R.F.A.

3-6-17.   Commanding Left Group   38th D.A.

ADDITION TO 38th DIVISIONAL ARTILLERY O.O. No.68.
———————————————————

Four 6" How. Batteries have been allotted to 38th Division front for bombardment on 3rd June.

The action of these Batteries will be as under :-

    Zero to Zero plus 15   CHEMIN TRENCH, MACKENSEN FARM and the area GALIFITZ FARM, CADDIE POINT, HOUSE 10, CACTUS POINT.

    Zero plus 15 to Zero plus 30.   All Batteries lift to CANE TRENCH and CANDLE TRENCH.

Copies to all recipients.

Issued at 9.50 p.m. 1/6/17.

[signature]

Major R.F.A.
A/Brigade Major, 38th Divisional Artillery.

APPENDIX 2.

Programme for "A"/121, "B"/121, Enfilade Section "B"/122, "D"/121 and "D"/122.

"A"/121 - Zero plus 15 to Zero plus 17. -
Front Line B.12.b.0.9. to C.7.c.85.75. (Smoke Shell).

Zero plus 17 to Zero plus 30. - "Spectators" - Shrapnel.

"B"/121 - Zero plus 15 to Zero plus 17. -
Front Line C.7.c.85.75 to C.7.d.97.15. (Smoke Shell).

Zero plus 17 to Zero plus 30. - "Spectators" - Shrapnel.

Enfilade Section "B"/122. Zero plus 15 to Zero plus 17.
Front Line C.14.a.85.00 to C.14.b.30.15. (Smoke Shell).

Zero plus 17 to Zero plus 30. - "Spectators" - Shrapnel.

"D"/121 (4) Zero to Zero plus 15. -
CAESAR SUPPORT and CAKE SUPPORT from C.8.c.1.0. to C.14.a.60.20.

Zero plus 15 to Zero plus 20 -
Northern half of "Blue" Line.

Zero plus 20 to Zero plus 25 -
Northern half of "Green" Line.

Zero plus 25 to Zero plus 30. -
Search CAESAR AVENUE North of MACKENSEN FARM.

"D"/121 (2) Zero to Zero plus 15. -
CADDIE TRENCH between KIEL COT and C.7.d.97.15.

Zero plus 15 to Zero plus 17. - CADDIE SUPPORT.

Zero plus 17 to Zero plus 30. - "Spectators".

"D"/122 (6) Zero to Zero plus 15 -
Front Line from C.7.d.97.15 to C.14.a.85.00.

Zero plus 15 to Zero plus 20. - Southern half of "Blue" Line.

Zero plus 20 to Zero plus 25 - Southern half of "Green" Line.

Zero plus 25 to Zero plus 30 - Search CALABASH AVENUE (but not within 200^x of "Green" Line) - 4 hows.

Search CHEMINS AVENUE (but not within 200^x of "Green" Line). - 2 hows.

The following/

APPENDIX 2. contd.

The following are likely places for Spectators. Group Commanders will make their own ~~arrangements~~ selections.

    (a) PILCKEM Neighbourhood.

        O.P's have been reported at :-

            C. 2.c.95.95. - House.
            C. 2.c.92.90. - -do-
            C. 2.c.20.60. - -do-
            C. 2.c.65.35. - Ruins of PILCKEM MILL.(a very extensive view obtainable from here). *A/121*

            C. 2.c.95.20. - Concrete O.P. in mound.

    (b)   C. 8.b.65.25. - MARSOUIN FARM.
            C. 8.b.95.10. - CRAB APPLE TREE.
            C. 8.c.33.10. - Camouflage willow tree.

    (c)   C.14.a.35.70.
            C.14.a.10.95.

    (d)   WOOD 15.
            C. 1.a.15.70.
            C. 1.a.50.50. (Tree.) *B/121*
            GENERAL FARM C.1.a.70.20. *D/121*
            C. 1.a.40.15.
            C. 1.a.35.05. (Tree.)

O.Ps.
No.1. B/121.
Joyeuse. D/121.
A/121 Doctor's Ho.
Representatives from Bty s at 12.30.

4. RATES OF FIRE.

    (a) 18-pdrs. of Creeping Barrage.

        Zero plus 15 to Zero plus 17.   5 rounds per gun per min.
        Zero plus 17 to Zero plus 30.   2   -do-   -do-

    (b) Remaining 18-pdrs.

        Zero plus 15 to Zero plus 17.   5 rounds per gun per min.
        Zero plus 17 to Zero plus 30.   **Bursts of Fire.**

    (c) 4.5" Hows.

        Zero to Zero plus 5.   1 round per How. per min.
        Zero plus 5 to Zero plus 13   1½   -do-   -do-
        Zero plus 13 to Zero plus 15.   2   -do-   -do-
        Zero plus 15 to Zero plus 30.   1   -do-   -do-

5. AMMUNITION.

    Zero plus 15 to Zero plus 17. - All 18-pdrs. - Smoke Shell.

    Zero plus 17 to Zero plus 30. - Creeping Barrage guns - T.S. with corrector to give 50% grazes.
    Remaining guns - T.S. with effective corrector.

6. Groups will arrange to have Observers stationed at suitable places to observe the hostile shelling, and will send in a report showing, as far as possible

    (a) Places where shells fall.
    (b) Time shelling starts and stops.
    (c) Calibre and nature of gun or howitzer.
    (d) True bearing from which fire comes.
    (e) Locality, true bearing, and time of machine gun fire.

7. From 12.50 p.m. to 3.10 p.m. on 3rd. June telephone and telegraphic communications in the Divisional Area will cease, with the exception of S.O.S. Messages, and messages between Artillery O.P's and Batteries. An operation PRIORITY message will have to be sent from Divisional H.Q. during this period.

    The following Code words will be used :-

    Zero postponed 1 hour   - BYSTANDER.

    Zero postponed to 4th. June - SKETCH.
    Zero to be at 3 p.m.   - GRAPHIC.
    Zero hour will be.... p.m. - ABSOLAM .. p.m.

8. A Divisional Staff Officer will attend at Right Infantry Bde. H.Q. to synchronize watches at 11 a.m. 3rd. June. Groups will send representatives for this purpose.

9. ACKNOWLEDGE.

2nd. June 1917.

J. T. Marston

Major R.F.A.
a/Brigade Major 38th. Divisional Artillery

Copies to:-

Right Group.
Left Group.
33th. Div. "G".
R.A., VIII Corps.
4th. Belgian Arty.
39th. D.A.

SECRET.   EG.37.

   Tasks for today June 1st as follows :-

1.   2" T.M's - CANAL AVENUE, concentrating between points
     B.12.b.9.7½ and C.7.a.15.50.
     Time of Commencement - 3.5 p.m.
     Ammunition : up to 200 rounds.
     Shoot will last about 2 hours.

2.   A/121. will provide covering fire on
     BABOON SUPPORT from B.6.d.00.85. to 60.50 ; B.6.d.72.55 to
     95.30., and CANAL AVENUE on points not engaged by T.M's. -
     400 rounds.

3.   B/121. will fire 400 rounds, half non-delay H.E. and half
     Shrapnel with at least 80% grazes on wire in front of
     CANAL DRIVE and parallel trench, so far as can be observed,
     West of HUDDLESTONE ROAD. Time as desired, but some to be
     reserved as covering fire for T.M's.

4.   D/121. (Section) 250 rounds on GDE BARRIERE HOUSE.

5.   A C K N O W L E D G E.

                                                          2/Lt. R.F.A.
1-6-17.   Adjutant Left Group 38th D.A.

SECRET.   R.A.VIII Corps No. RA/746/55.
          R.A.38th Division NO.G.S.2190.

38th Division.
39th Division.
55th Division.
VIIIth Corps Heavy Arty.
21st Squadron R.F.C.
----

1.   Harassing fire will be kept up on back areas
and approaches by day as well as night from now onwards
between the hours of 10 a.m. and 5.p.m. - unless aeroplanes
are working.
            When any harassing fire is likely to impede
aerial observation between these hours, O.C., 21st Squadron
will wire direct to Divisional Artilleries concerned.

2.   Destruction of hostile Observation Posts is to
start on June 4th.   From then onwards all known and
suspected O.P's should be destroyed.

                         SD/. C.GELDARD Major. for
                                    Brig.-General R.A.,
2/6/17.   for B.G., General Staff, VIIIth Corps.

Copies to -

VIIIth Corps "G".
B.G.R.A., 38th Division.
B.G.R.A., 39th Division.
B.G.R.A., 55th Division.

-2-

O.C.
    Right Group.
    Left Group.   "URGENT"
-----------------   -----------

                    For information and necessary action.

                                  [signature]

                                              Major R.F.A.
2/6/17.   A/Brigade Major, 38th Divisional Artillery.

Copy No. 10

38th. DIVISIONAL ARTILLERY OPERATION ORDER No. 65.

1. A bombardment of the German Front system opposite the VIII Corps front will be carried out to-morrow 3rd. June by the Corps Heavy Artillery and 4.5". Hows. of Divisional Artilleries.

   The Bombardment will start at Zero and finish at Zero plus 30. From Zero plus 15 to Zero plus 30 two practice barrages will be carried out, one by the 39th. D.A. and 55th. D.A. on the WIELTJE front and one by the 38th. Divisional Artillery on the KRUPP SALIENT.

2. The action of the 38th. D.A. will be as follows :-

   The Creeping Barrage will be carried out according to the attached tracing (Appendix 1.) by :-

   "A"/122 - 6 guns.
   "B"/122. - 4 "
   "C"/122 - 4 "
   "C"/121 - 6 "

   For the first two minutes of the barrage (Zero plus 15 to Zero plus 17.) Smoke Shell will be used by all 18-pdrs. During this period "A"/121, "B"/121 and enfilade section "B"/122 will fire on the front line on the flanks of the barrage: from Zero plus 17 till Zero plus 30 those guns will deal with "Spectators."

   Details of their action and that of "D"/121 and "D"/122 are shown in Appendix 2.

3. Time Table is as under :-

Zero to Zero plus 15	Hows. on Front and Support line.
Zero plus 15. Barrage opens	(18-pdrs. on Front Line. (4.5" Hows. on Blue Line.
Zero plus 17.	"A"/121, "B"/121, 1 section "B"/122 lift to "Spectator" Targets.
Zero plus 20.	Barrage starts to creep forward - 4.5" Hows. lift to Green Line.
Zero plus 25.	Hows. lift to Communication Trenches.
Zero plus 27.	Barrage reaches Green Line.
Zero plus 29.	Barrage drops back to Blue Line.
Zero plus 30.	Fire ceases.

R.(A) Contd.   O.O. 53. Sheet 3.

4.5" Howitzers.

"E"/121. (2 Hows).   - 1 How. - FARM 14.
Left Group RIVERSIDGES.   1 "   - C.7.c.60.75.

"D"/122. (3 Hows)   - 1 How. - C.7.d. 5. 4.
DAWSONS CORNER.   1 "   - KIEL COT.
                          1 "   - CACTUS POINT.

Rate of fire for Howitzers - 3 rounds per gun per minute during this period.

Heavy T.M. will fire at CACTUS JUNCTION.

2 Medium T.M's. - Will fire at C.7.c.15.85. and C.7.a.27.00.

        11.32.p.m. to 11.47.p.m.

"B"/121. 3 Guns.   )
(Left Group)   ) - Will switch to the left and enfilade as
"C"/122. 4 Guns.   )   follows :-
(C.21.b.4.5.)   )

"E"/121. 3 Guns. - From FARM 14 to C.7.b.00.05.

"D"/122. 4 Guns. - From C.7.b.00.05. to CACTUS POINT.

Objectives of all other 18-Pdrs, all 4.5" Howitzers and Trench Mortars, will remain the same as in previous period.

Rates of fire.
        18-Pdrs - 3 rounds per gun per minute.
        4.5" Hows. - 2 rounds per gun per minute.

Ammunition. As in previous period.

All fire will cease at 11.47.p.m.

An Officer from "D"/122 will be at SPIES NEST O.P. during the operation in communication with Group Hd.Qrs.
There will be telephone communication between our new front line in C.7.d. to POST 31 - C.13.b.35.38.

4.) The following code words will be used :-

        DIAMONDS   - Prisoners.
        CLUBS.   - More Artillery fire required.
        SPADES.   - Identification.
        HEARTS.   - Raiding party returned.

Prefixes as follows will be sent before the above Code words

A. For 10th. Welsh Raid.   P P P

B. For 13th. Welsh Raid.   K K K

5.) All Guns will be carefully laid on these lines and all fuzes checked, procedure for all guns being carefully explained.

                                        W E Rudder
                                        Lieut. Colonel. R.F.A.

8th. June 1917.   Commanding Right Group. 38th. D. A.

SECRET.   EG.69.

                Action by Left Group R.A. tomorrow 9th June will
be as follows, starting at 2 p.m.

(1) A/121 will continue to cut wire in front of CANAL AVENUE.

(2) 2" T.M's. will bombard the communication trench B.6.d.55.00.
to the West Corner of ARTILLERY WOOD.   Up to 150 rounds.

(3) B/121. 200 rounds H.E. on CARIBOO LANE   GC.d.c.7.9. ; GC.d.b.5.52.

(4) A/121. (4 guns) 200 H.E. on CARIBOO TRENCH GC.d.a.3.3.
GC.d.c.7.9.

(5) D/121 (section) 1 How. GC.d.a.30.32. 50 rounds.
                      1 How. GC.d.a.G.D.   50 rounds.

(6) ACKNOWLEDGE.

                                                    Rowie
                                                            2/Lt. R.F.A.
8.6.17.   Adjutant Left Group 38th D.A.

Copies to:
O.C. Left M.T.M. Group
    D.T.M.O.
    115th Infantry Brigade.
    A/121.
    B/121.
    D/121.

S E C R E T.
                                                                EG.61.

(1) Medium Trench Mortars will bombard the trench area B.12.b.92.72 – 90.78 – C.7.a.05.90. – 10.78. – 05.65. starting at 11.30 a.m. tomorrow 8th, up to 150 rounds.

(2) A/121. wire cutting section will cut lanes in the wire in front of CANAL AVENUE. 300 rounds. The best view of this is from DOCTORS' HOUSE.

(3) B/121. Enfilade C.1.d.00.30. to C.2.a.40.20. 250 rounds.

(4) B/121. C.1.d.30.55. – 55.70. 100 rounds.

(5) A/121. 4 guns will fire bursts of fire on CANCER TRENCH (H.F. Scheme 3.)

(6) A C K N O W L E D G E.

Powell.

2/Lt. R.F.A.

O.O.35. Sheet 4.

Copies to:-
    O. C. "B"/121. (Left Group)
    O. C. "C"/121. (2)
    O. C. "D"/121.
    O. C. "D"/121. (Left Group)
    O. C. "A"/122.
    O. C. "B"/122.
    O. C. "C"/122.
    O. C. "D"/122. (2)
    Right Group T.M's.
    H. Q., 114th. Inf. Bde.
    O. C. Left Group 38th. D.A.
    O. C. 13th. Welsh Regt.(2)
    O. C. 10th. Welsh Regt.(2)
    H. Q., 38th. Div. Arty. (2)
    File and War Diary. (2)

WAR DIARY.

A/121 Battery R.F.A.   29th to 31st Aug. 1916.

Place	Date	Time		Appendix
ELVERDIN -GHE	29th	noon	The old A/120 R.F.A. was reorganised & became a 6 gun battery. The right section of B/120 was taken over, & the new battery called A/121. The battery came into action at 7pm & took over the guns of C/121, & one section being about 700' in advance of the other two.	
	30th / 31st		Registration.	

MD Townsend
Capt.
Comdg A/121 R.F.A.

1-9-16

Army Form C. 2118.

WAR DIARY
or
INTELLIGENCE SUMMARY

(Erase heading not required.)

121 Bde. R.A.
October 1917

Vol 2

Place	Date	Hour	Summary of Events and Information	Remarks and references to Appendices
ARMENTIÈRES	Oct 1917		The disposition of the Brigade have not changed since the last Diary. Batteries 17th 121 Bde., plus the 376 Battery, 169 AFA Bde., make up the Left Group 9th Divisional Sub-Group, the 115th Inf. Bde. is in the line. No major operation has taken place. Our active minor operation have been carried out, including a local bombardment of the enemy defenses in C 29, a bombardment in connection with firing of gas bombs by Special Coys. R.E., also on C.29, and a retaliatory shoot-on tank cross further on. Shelling of BAC ST. MAUR on 17th October. Wheeltapping, by 6" Hows 6" and 2" trench mortars, 4.5" Hows, 18 Pdrs. has been carried out during the last half of the month on the long stationary line in IIIa, in preparation for a raid proposed by 115th Infantry Bde. The Batteries in the Group which are doing this are 376 Bde., B/121 and D/121. B/121 has a gun moved forward to this purpose in I 9 a. A/121 has also done some wirecutting as a division in C.17c. A good deal of hostile counter-battery work has been undertaken. At our F.O.B.As. batteries have been heavily shelled at one time another. The line guns of A/121 which are near FLEURBAIX F.M. in C 14 b have had to be moved to positions in C 14 c. Casualties in the Brigade during the month have been practically nil. R.S.M. Blenkey has been posted into R.S.M. Hills who took his discharge in September.	Shepherds

G.P. MacLellan
Lieut Col C.R.A.
Comdg. 121 Bde R.A.

SECRET.   Copy No. 9

LEFT GROUP – 38th D.A. Operation Order No. 1.   6th Oct. 1917.
_____

1. Left Group R.A. will carry out a local bombardment in the neighbourhood of CENTAUR TRENCH, LANE, ROW, CRESCENT, etc, in conjunction with 91st H.A.G. on Monday 8th inst.

2. Targets will be as follows :–
A/121. (6 guns)   C.29.a.65.42. – b.00.22.
                  C.29.d.00.67. – 60.60. (trench)
                  C.29.d.00.57. – 48.00. (trench)
B/121. (4 guns)   C.29.a.65.42. – 23.c.88.00.
                  C.29.a.78.30. – 23.d.08.00.
                  C.29.a.96.22. – b.15.35.
                  C.29.a.96.22. – b.05.55.
C/121. (1 gun)   C.29.d.05.72. – 62.90.
       (3 guns) Search and sweep area C.29.c.62.62. – a.42.00. –
                                       – b.08.00. – d.05.72.
376th Bty. (3 guns) Search and sweep area C.29.a.42.00. – 65.42. –
                                          – 96.22. – b.08.00.
           (1 gun) C.29.b.15.35. – 78.30.
D/121. (2 Hows.) CENTAUR CRESCENT.
       (1 How.) C.29.c.88.70.

3. The 91st H.A.G. is co-operating by bombarding enemy's front trench C.29.c.48.80. – a.48.25. and the trench junctions C.29.c.78.85., C.29.a.68.12., C.29.a.78.30., and C.29.a.96.22.

4. The 2" T.M. will cut wire between C.29.c.90.38. – 60.65.

5. Watches will be synchronized at Left Group Headquarters at 6 p.m. on 7th inst.

6. Zero hour will be notified later.

7. Ammunition – 18 pdrs. 70 rounds per gun all H.E., except C/121. and 376th Bty. which will fire half T.S.
4.5" Hows. 100 rounds per How.
T.M.'s Up to 100 rounds.

8. Fire will cease at Zero plus 2 hours.

9. PLEASE ACKNOWLEDGE.

                                          Lieut. Colonel R.A.
                              Commanding LEFT GROUP – 38th D.A.

Copy No. 1.   A/121.
        2.   B/121.
        3.   C/121.
        4.   D/121.
        5.   376th Bty. R.F.A.
        6.   115th Infantry Bde.
        7.   38th D.A.
        8.   D.T.M.O.
        9.   War Diary.
       10.   File.
       11.   91st H.A.G.

E.L.G. 6/10.

1. The 2" T.M's will fire on the Point of the Salient at I.11.a.31.22. They will start at 3 p.m. today and fire for about 2 hours.

2. Covering fire will be provided as follows :-
B/121. Trench I.11.c.80.22. - I.11.a.62.22.
376 Bty. Trench I.11.a.62.22. - I.11.b.11.99.
D/121. Suspected O.P. at C.18.c.5?.80. LA HONGRIE FARM.

18 pdrs. will also fire a few rounds on Front line trenches corresponding to the above targets in SUPPORT TRENCH.

3. AMMUNITION. 18 pdrs. 400 rounds per battery.
   How. 20 rounds.

4. RATE OF FIRE. 18 pdrs. Bursts of fire will be employed of varying length and at varying intervals.
   Hows. will fire occasional rounds.

5. F.O.O's will watch for the start of the T.M. Shoot, and will then start covering fire. They will stop as soon as the T.M. stops. It must be understood that the T.M's may not start precisely at 3 p.m., and it is very likely they may stop long before 5 p.m.

6. All hostile MINNIE activity in this area will be reported at once to this Office.

7. PLEASE ACKNOWLEDGE BY WIRE.

Lieut. Colonel R.A.
13th Oct.1917. Commanding Left Group :- 35th D. A.

Left Group 28DIV — AD 307.

1. The following programme will be carried out tomorrow 20th Oct. at 3 pm.
    A/121.   I 6c 28.85 – 83.00.
    B/121.   INANE AVENUE   I 12a 55.98 – 6a 30.98.
    C/121.   INANE DRIVE.   I 5b 65.00 – 6a 40.00 and I 6b 0.0 – 90.04
    376 Bty. Farm at I 6a 60.05.
    D/121.   INANE SWITCH   I 6c 28.85 – 12a 85.98.

2. Rate of Fire.
    First 5 min.   18 pdrs.   3 rounds per gun per min.
                   4.5" How   2   "   "   "
    Second 5 min. 18 pdrs.   1   "   "   "
                   4.5 Hows   1   "   "   "

3. Ammunition – 18 pdrs – 75% HE.

4. At 4.15 pm. all guns & howitzers which can bear will fire 10 rounds gunfire on strong point at C 12c 2.2. All HE.

5. Watches will be synchronized by telephone.

6. A/121. will continue wirecutting at C 17c 85.60.
   Ammunition – up to 200 rounds.

7. This will cut wire opposite the EPINETTE Salient commencing at 3 pm.

8. Acknowledge.

Left Group. 38 DA
                                                                AD 306

1. A combined shoot will be carried out this afternoon
(18th October) on the points in the back area opposite the
centre of the Divisional Front, in retaliation for enemy
shelling of BAC S. MAUR yesterday.

2. Time — 3.30 p.m. — 5 p.m.

3. Left Group will cooperate as follows —

   B/121 — all available guns   PREMESQUES (I.24)
          remainder   PERENCHIES

   376 Bty. any available guns   PREMESQUES
             remainder as available PERENCHIES and suitable points
                                    between LA PRÉVÔTE & PERENCHIES.

   A/121   all available guns   LA PRÉVÔTE

   D/121   all available hows — PREMESQUES if possible,
                                   otherwise PERENCHIES.

   C/121   available guns   —   PERENCHIES to LA PRÉVÔTE.

4. C/121 + D/121 should carry out the programme of covering fire already detailed,
D/121 using one how only and firing 40 rounds. C/121 will
take part in the combined shoot as far as possible while not
engaged in covering fire. D/121 should make every effort to
get as many hows as possible to bear on the PREMESQUES and
PERENCHIES targets.

5. Ammunition.
   B/121 ⎫
   376 Bty ⎬ 20 rounds per gun.
   A/121 ⎪
   D/121 ⎭

   C/121   10 rounds per gun.

   All HE except B/121 which will fire 50 rounds incendiary,
   as many as possible or all of these latter to fire into
   PREMESQUES.
                                        Bruce Campbell
6. Acknowledge by phone.   Capt. Left Group.

Hollsiongs 38DD

MOST   AD 208

1. At 9.5 pm tonight (30/4)

D/f21 will fire all the gas-shell on hand on CENSOR FM and neighbourhood in an effective rate according to the instructions for obtaining the proper concentration.

2. (On ...) 576 Bty will fire 3 salvoes each, all H.E., on the [illegible] CENSOR FM. between 9.5 pm & 9.30 pm to catch personnel in the open.

3. [illegible]

29.10.17
Rev. to D/f21
G/121

Secret. Left Group 38DA. Copy No. 6
Operation Order No. 2. 28th Oct. 1917.

1. No 1 Special Coy. R.E. are firing gas bombs at the following targets this evening, 28th October, or the first subsequent favourable evening.
   (a.) Distillery I.27.a & b.
   (b.) WEZ MACQUART
   (c.) Enemy defences in C.29.a, b, & c.

2. Left Group will cooperate on target (c) in accordance with attached Schedule.

3. The bombardment will last about 15 minutes and will commence at 7 pm if the wind is favourable; if not, at 9.30 pm.

4. The following code words will be used:—
   ADAM = gas bombardment – Zero 7 pm tonight.
   EVE =   "   "   –   " 9.30pm "
   The above will be telegraphed from this office not later than 3 hours before Zero.
   CAIN = gas bombardment will not take place tonight.

5. Watches will be synchronized at D/121 at 4.15 pm to day.

6. ACKNOWLEDGE.

Howell Capt. R.F.A.
Adjt. Left Group. 38DA.

Copy No 1 A/121
      2 B/121   No. 6. File
      3 C/121   7. War Diary.
      4 376 Bty.
      5 D/121

SECRET.

~~PROPOSED~~ ARTILLERY ACTION DURING GAS PROJECTION.

"A"
Zero to +3; and +16 to +18; and +23 to +26.

A/121. 2 guns CENTRAL SUPPORT
        2 ,,   ,, TRENCH
        2 ,,   CENTAUR SUPPORT

B/121. 2 guns C.29.c.79.98. - b.08.58.
        1 ,,   CENSUS SUPPORT
        1 ,,   CENTRAL SWITCH.

C/121. 2 guns. Tramway C.29.b.00.25. - 45.72.
        1 ,,   C.29.d.07.74. - 40.86.
        1 ,,   C.29.b.00.20. - 25.34.

376 Bty. 1 gun C.29.b.00.22. - 18.38.
         1 ,,   C.29.b.00.60. - 22.98.
         2 ,,   C.23.d.02.52. - 30.80.

D/121.   I.5.b.62.95.
         C.29.b.22.98.
         C.29.a.98.23.

"B"
+3 to +16 and +56 to +59.

A/121. 2 guns I.5.b.67.85. - 6.a.70.00.
        2 ,,   I.5.b.63.72. - 6.a.50.13.
        2 ,,   Tramway C.29.d.05.74. - 30.c.18.45

B/121. 2 guns C.30.c.28.45. - a.72.00.
        2 ,,   C.29.b.80.90. - 24.c.17.24.

C/121. 2 guns C.29.b.45.72. 80.90.
        1 ,,   C.29.b.45.42. - 30.a.18.62.
        1 ,,   C.29.b.95.02. - 30.a.42.32.

376 Bty. 2 guns C.29.d.50.60. - 30.c.50.83.
         2 ,, C.29.b.60.33. - 30.a.42.47.

D/121. No change.

Rates of fire

Zero to +3	18 pdrs 4 rounds per gun per minute.
+16 to +18	4-5" Hows. 3 ,, ,, ,,
+23 to +26	18 pdrs. 3 ,, ,, ,,
+56 to +59	4-5" Hows. 2 ,, ,, ,,
+3 to +16.	18 pdrs and 4.5"Hows. 1 ,, ,, ,,

SECRET.

38th (Welsh) DIVISION ORDER NO 146.

27th October 1917.

1. No 1 Special Company R.E. will fire Gas Bombs at the following targets on the evening of the 28th October, or the first subsequent evening on which the wind is favourable.

    (a) Neighbourhood of the DISTILLERY I.27.a. and b.
    (b) WEZ MACQUART.
    (c) Enemy defences in C.29.a. and part of C.29.b. & c.

2. Artillery and Machine Guns which bear on these targets and the vicinity will, open fire on trenches and tracks during and after the gas bombardment as arranged by Infantry Brigades and Artillery Group Commanders and (as regards Machine Guns) by the D.M.G.O.

3. The gas bombardment will last for about 15 minutes and will commence at 5.30 p.m. if the wind is favourable, or if not at 9.30 p.m. If the wind is still unfavourable at 9.30 p.m. the bombardment will be postponed until the next evening.

4. The following code words will be used :-

    ADAM = Gas bombardment Zero 7.0 p.m. tonight.
    EVE = Gas bombardment Zero 9.30 p.m. tonight.

    The above words will telegraphed from this office not later than four hours before Zero.

    CAIN = Gas bombardment will not take place this evening.

5. Orders to be issued that posts which are in the line of fire of the 4" Stokes Mortars will wear box respirators from 5 minutes before Zero for twenty-five minutes, to guard against risk of prematures.

6. Infantry Brigade Commanders will be responsible for conveying the Orders as given in para.4 to the Sections Special Coy. R.E. who are in position on their part of the line.

SD. R.S.FOLJET Major, for
Lieut Colonel.
General Staff, 38th (Welsh) Division.

O.C.
RIGHT GROUP.
LEFT GROUP.
CENTRE GROUP.
D.T.M.O.
8th Divisional Artillery . For information.

Forwarded for information and necessary action.

Captain R.F.A.
27.10.17. a/Brigade Major, 38th Divisional Artillery.

SECRET.   115th INFANTRY BRIGADE B.M. 5090

BRIGADE ORDER.

                                                                  targets
1. No.1 Special Coy. R.E. are firing gas bombs at the following/
   on the evening of the 28th October, or the first subsequent
   evening on which wind is favourable:-

   (a) Neighbourhood of the Distillery, I.27.a.& b.

   (b) WEZ MACQUART

   (c) Enemy defences in C.29.a., and part of C.29.b.& c.

2. Target (c) above, which is on the front of the 115th Infantry
   Brigade, is being engaged by B & D Sections No.1 Special
   Coy., R.E. from positions about C.28.d.8.6. and C.28.b.8.9.

3. Left Group R.F.A. will co-operate by firing on selected enemy
   trenches and tracks at intervals from Zero to Zero plus
   59 mins. in accordance with programme drawn up by O.C. Left
   Group.

4. Co-operation by Machine Guns is being arranged by D.M.G.O.

5. The gas bombardment will last about 15 minutes, and will
   commence at 7.0 p.m. if the wind is favourable, or, if
   not, at 9-30 p.m.. If the wind is still unfavourable
   at 9.30 p.m., the bombardment will be postponed until the
   next evening.

6. The following code words will be used:-

   ADAM = Gas bombardment - ZERO 7 pm. to-night
   EVE =   "   "   -   " 9.30 pm. to-night.

   The above words will be telegraphed from this office to all
   concerned not later than 3½ hours before ZERO.

   CAIN = Gas bombardment will not take place this evening.

7. Garrisons of posts Nos. 1 & 2, 8, 10, 11 & 12 will wear box
   respirators from 5 minutes before ZERO hour for 25 minutes, to
   guard against risk of prematures.
   Garrison of post No. 1 will withdraw to post No. 8 ten minutes
   before ZERO hour, and return to No. 1 post at ZERO plus 30 mins.

8. Lieut. J.D.OUSEY i/c B. & D. Sections No. 1 Special Coy.,R.E.
   will remain at Left Battalion H.Q. (GLOUCESTER AV.) during the
   operation.
   C.O., Left Battalion will be responsible for communicating to
   Lieut. OUSEY the orders as given in para. 6.
   Lieut. OUSEY will be responsible for transmitting these orders
   to B. & D. Sections in the line.

9. Watches will be synchronized at Left Battalion H.Q. at 3 pm. 28th
   October. Each
   One Officer/from Left Group, R.F.A., No. 1 Special Coy.,R.E.,
   115 M.G.Company, 176 M.G.Company and Left Battalion, will attend
   at that hour at Left Battalion H.Q.

10. Orders given in para. 6 will be wired from Brigade H.Q. to -
    Left Group, R.F.A.
    Right & Left Battalions in the line,
    115 M.G.Company,
    176 M.G.Company,
    23rd Infy. Brigade, 8th Division.

11. ACKNOWLEDGE.
    28.10.1917   R.H.Stone
                          A/BRIGADE MAJOR, 115th Infy. Brigade.
                                                       Captain,

Army Form C. 2118.

WAR DIARY
or
INTELLIGENCE SUMMARY
(Erase heading not required.)

/21 Bde R.F.A.

November 1917

Place	Date	Hour	Summary of Events and Information	Remarks and references to Appendices
ARMENTIÈRES	Nov. 1917 1/8		Formation of Batteries and Headquarters as before work. After an interval of some time taken by 97th R Bk. On night 8/9 Nov. the 376th R Bk. left the group; the chief event of the month was the Raid, which was carried out on the enemy lines in I.11.a by 18th Scots in the early morning of Nov. 9th. The Raid was successful. Our casualties were comparatively light considering that the lighter half slept in an hour. Some retaliation in Counter Battery work was very slight. The enemy 5.9 Hows. 10 days after spent either enemy or action & field guns & trench mortars & 6" Hows. He was able to be captured. Their were also well cut, but short outputs hits. Wiring parties have been put on frequently. Sometimes by the S.P.V. Fort Raid. The group was reinforced by the 59th R.B.A. (Horse Thomson) - 3 10/11 Batteries of 7.4. Show Hs. (4 hrs.) Neighbor Litt. action on the night 5/6 Nov. as Place - A/59 at 13 C 2.4. 10. N/59 Br. 18 C 9.6. C/59 - 2 guns. C at 3.0. 2 guns - C 26 f. 8.9. 2 guns to conflict 15/17. D/59. C 26 C 5.3. Causality after the Raid. This trench pulled their up and after completing excellent work, their wished to remain here; the retaliation of the group thence. Retaliation heavy & 24/11/17. The enemy attacked a raid on our trenches in I.5. This on hours for several days by cutting wing on the first plan & alface our wire-front, and was accompanied by a heavy Tin. & artillery barrage. His were were - The fire that when intended by trench mortars of .... Heavy Charge it in N.M.Ls .... our troops Combs Polis with other enemy had been frequently attacked almost may by the enemy. The .... their in 14/11/17. Major His Townsend (H/59) had formally left commanding the group. Forward or further .... above effort here also on 4 months leave .... Length of fire short are attached.	See Appendix "Raid" attached.
	24			

Signed ....
Major RFA
Comdg. 121 Bde R.F.A.
1/12/17

SECRET.

LEFT GROUP :- 38th D.A. Operation Order No. 3.   Nov.6th, 1917
....

1. The 10th Batt. S.W. Borderers is raiding the enemy in INCANDESCENT TRENCH and SUPPORT tomorrow night 7/8th Nov. Zero hour will be notified later.

The Raiding party will be formed up in NO MAN'S LAND, just in front of our own wire by Zero hour.

The points of entry are between I.11.a.45.32. and I.5.c.70.05. and after the entry has been effected, Blocks are being established at the following points viz:-
I.11.a.83.25.
I.11.a.60.37.
I.11.b.08.80.
I.11.b.02.85.
I.5.c.70.05.
and flanking parties in NO MAN'S LAND at
I.11.a.28.32.
I.5.c.60.12.

2. The Left Group Artillery programme and one amendment thereto have been issued to all concerned.

Special care is to be taken that the first lift of the Creeping barrage shall be far enough beyond the enemy front line to allow of the raiders climbing out of the front trench on their way to the Support Line.

3. The Left Group M.T.M's will co-operate with one 6" Newton gun each on a suspected T.M. at I.11.c.95.50; a suspected M.G. at I.5.b.25.25.; and CENSORS NOSE.

4. The following O.P's will be manned by an Officer found as shown against them, on the night 7/8th Nov. from Zero - 1 Hour until the order "Break Off" is given from this Office, when normal night manning will be resumed viz ::-
EREWHON or NOWHERE by A/121.
BRENTWOOD   by D/121.

5. Liaison Officers will be found as follows on the night 7/8th Nov.-
Right Battalion Headquarters.....D/121.
Right Battalion Advanced Headquarters at Centre Co. Headquarters I.10.b.50.85...........B/121.
Left Battalion Headquarters..........C/121.
An experienced Officer is to be sent in each case.

The Liaison Officers with Right Battalion will keep Left Group R.A. informed as to the progress of the Operation; reports of hostile shelling are of the utmost importance, and will be sent in by Liaison Officers and O.P's as it occurs.

An Officer from Group H.Qrs is being sent to O.P. Exchange during the Operation.

-2-

This Officer and the Liaison Officer at Right Battalion Advanced Headquarters may return to their Units after the conclusion of the Operation.

6. The Signal that the barrage is to be intensified will be: 10 Green Very Lights sent up by Raiding Party; on seeing this Signal Liaison and O.P. Officers will report it at once to O.P. Exchange (G.O.5.) and then to Group by the Code word "GINGER"; on receipt of this Code word, batteries will increase rate of fire as follows :-

18 pdrs.   4 rounds per gun per minute for 5 minutes, then 2 rounds per gun per minute for 5 minutes, then return to normal rates.   B/59. will stop searching and return to the back of the box.

4-5" Hows.   3 rounds per gun per minute for 5 minutes, then 2 rounds per gun per minute for 5 minutes, then return to the normal rate.   A number of Green Lights which may not total 10 must be taken as a call for "GINGER".   This signal must not be confused with Blue Light Signals which do not affect the Artillery.

7. The following Code words will be employed :-
Raiding party has entered enemy's front line...... JAM.
  ,,   ,,   ,,   ,, Support Line....... STRAWBERRY.
  ,,   ,, has re-entered our line............ MARMALADE.

8. Watches will be synchronized at D/121. Officers Mess at 9.30 p.m. 7th inst.

9. A C K N O W L E D G E.

Lieut. Colonel R.A.
Commanding Left Group ;- 38th D.A.

Scott Wynne.   AD 046.

Extract from Counter Battery Office
XI Corps Operation Order No. 34.

1. Counter Battery Work (night of 7/8 Nov. 1917).

   Batteries of 91st. HAG. + three 4.5" Hows
   38th DA. will neutralise hostile batteries as
   under -

   4.5 Hows Left Group 38 DA. on J 1 b 65.65.

2. Rate of Fire -
   Zero to Zero + 15 . . . . RAPID
   Zero + 15 onwards . . . . SLOW (Ready
                                      to increase to Rapid)

6. Ammunition.
   4.5" Hows & 60 pdrs will fire
   Gas shell if weather conditions are favourable.

                            [signature]
                            O/C. Left Group. 38 DA

7.11.17.

/ Continued /.

9.
Zero. Will be notified later.

Issued at 5pm.
5/11/17.

Lieut. Colonel R.A.
C.B.S.O. XIth Corps.

Copies to:-
91st H.A. Group .... 9 copies.
38th Div. "G" 1
38th D.A. 3
R.A. XI Corps 1
H.A. XI Corps 1
No.7 Group, 1st F.S.Coy. 1
File 2

Extract sent to D/171   *Left Group*

SECRET.   Counter Battery Office, XIth Corps.

Operation Order No. 34.

1. Intention. On the night of 7/8 November 1917, 115th Brigade will carry out a raid on German Front and Support Lines roughly between points I.11.a.6.3 and I.5.c.7.0.

2. F.A. Support. Left Group 38th D.A.

3. Duration. Operations will probably last about 1¼ hours.

4. Counter Battery Work. Batteries 91st H.A.G. + three 4.5" Hows. 38th D.A. will neutralize Hostile Batteries as under:-

    ADEPT   (6" How.) on H.B. DA.65 and J.3.b.10.55

    AFRESH (8" How.) on JC.20

    ADMIRE (6" Hows.) on JA.13, 27, 45, and J.14.c.2.8

    ABDUL   (60 Pdrs.) on JA.16 (and J.14.c.45.40)

    ABBESS (60 Pdrs.) on JA.15

    ADJUST (6" Hows.) on OB.12 and 17

    ADVISE (6" Hows.) on ID.15, 16, 17.

    4.5" Hows. Centre Group, 38th DA. on ID.8

    Left Group, 38th D.A. on J.1.b.65.65

5. Rate of Fire. Zero to Zero + 15 .... RAPID.

    Zero + 15 onwards .... SLOW (Ready to increase to RAPID.)

6. Ammunition. 4.5" Hows. and 60 Pdrs. will fire Gas Shell if weather conditions are favourable.

7. Communication. During operations the Left Group 38th D.A. will be plugged through direct to 91st H.A. Group and will keep 91st Group informed as to intensity of enemy artillery fire on front trenches or back areas (battery positions etc).
    91st H.A.G. will take action accordingly and inform C.B. Office.

8. Feint. A camouflage raid will be in operation about I.21.d. at same hour.

/ Continued /

Adjutant
Left Group

SECRET

Following is scheme for communications for night 7th/8th. You will have a direct line from your office to GO5 and to GO8. Communication with all OP's, O.C. Battalion and following batteries of 59th Bde RFA through GO5.

       A/59
       C/59
       D/59.

B/59 through HG14.

Communication with all 121st Bde RFA batteries and 376 Bty through GO8.

In conjunction with 115 Bde Signals, lamp communication will be established from my visual station at B.30.d.65.35 with Right Batt. H.Q. and Erquinghem. There is a direct line from this visual station to GO8.

O.C. Battalion will have a line to O.C. raid. A line will also be run to German front line & a telephone installed there. In addition to this a Power Buzzer will work from German F.L. to an amplifier in our lines.

Lt RFA
Sigs Left Group.

A.D. 045.

SECRET.

1. In view of the very long march which the 59th Bde R.F.A. has to make tomorrow (8th) the guns of its batteries will be pulled out after the Raid tonight (7th/8th Nov.) and taken to 59th Bde Battery Wagon Lines by teams and limbers to be detailed by 121st Bde Batteries.

2. 121st Bde Wagon Line Officers will arrange to have the teams and limbers at the guns of 59th Bde at 4.30 a.m. tomorrow 8th, by which time the situation should be quiet.

   N.C.O's i/c teams must, however, be guided by circumstances when bringing them up.

3. Batteries of 59th Brigade R.F.A. will each arrange to send a guide tonight to the Wagon Line of that 121st Bde Battery whose teams are to pull out their own guns. He will guide the teams to the guns.

   O.C. C/59. will arrange to send one guide from each of his 3 positions to A/121. Wagon Line.

   When the guns have been pulled out, they will be guided by the 59th Bde gunners to the Wagon Lines of the latter, three of which are in the neighbourhood of NOUVEAU MONDE, and one at A/121. Wagon Line.

4. Teams and Limbers will be furnished as follows :-
A/121.   6 teams for C/59. at C.14.b.75.04. (2 guns)
                              C.26.b.83.87. (2 guns)
                              I.8.b.20.20. (B/121. position 2 Guns)
B/121.   6 teams for B/59. at I.8.c.95.55. (6 guns)
C/121.   6 teams for A/59. at I.3.c.40.03. (6 guns)
D/121.   4 teams for D/59. at C.26.c.42.32. (4 hows)

5. The 121st Bde Wagon Lines are all near L'EPINETTE, N. of ERQUINGHEM.
A/121.........H.3.b.6.8.
B/121.........B.27.d.7.8.
C/121.........B.27.d.1.6.
D/121.........B.26.d.3.2.

                                                    Powell
                                                         Capt. R.F.A.
7-11-17.   Adjutant Left Group   38th D.A.

Copies to : 121st Bde R.F.A. Batteries.
              ,,   ,,   ,, Wagon Lines.
            59th Bde R.F.A. Batteries.
            59th Bde R.F.A. Headquarters.

SECRET.

LEFT GROUP 38th D.A. INSTRUCTIONS No 7.

A shoot will be carried out tomorrow as under :-

A/121   6 guns   C.23.b.40.15. - 90.03.
B/121   3 guns   C.23.d.40.80. - 60.93.
C/121   3 guns   C.23.d.60.95. - C.24.a.10.01.
97th Battery   3 guns   C.23.b.20.13. - 25.35.
D/121   (1 how)   C.23.b.40.15.
        (1 how)   C.23.b.30.12.
        (1 how)   C.23.d.43.82.

TRENCH MORTARS.

    CENSOR SUPPORT. - C.23.d.27.98. - C.23.a.50.45.

AMMUNITION.

    4.5" hows   20 rounds per gun.
    18 pdrs   20 rounds per gun.
    (All Non-delay H.E.)
    T.M.   100 rounds

TIME   2 p.m. to 3 p.m.

A few rounds should be fired beforehand in registration.

                                  Major R.F.A.
27/11/1917.   Commanding LEFT GROUP, 38th D.A.

Copies to
    A/121
    B/121
    C/121
    D/121
    97th Battery
    115th Infantry Brigade.
    38th D.A.
    D.T.M.O.

SECRET.   R.A., 38th Division No.G.S.496.

LEFT GROUP.
D.T.M.O.

1. As a retaliation for the enemy shelling of our trenches in the Left Sector early this morning the Divisional Commander wishes a concentrated combined shoot carried out on INANE DRIVE from I.5.d.45.90 to I.6.a.40.00, and farm I.6.a.02.60 tomorrow afternoon.

2. O.C. Left Group will arrange all details in connection with G.O.C. Left Infantry Brigade and D.T.M.O.

3. All Trench Mortars which can reach this target will co-operate but no T.M's will be moved from their present sites.

4. O.C. 91st H.A.G. has been asked to co-operate.

5. The shoot is to be entirely destructive and 18-pdrs will use delay H.E. only.

6. If visibility permits the fire will, where possible, be directed by observation.

7. Ammunition allowance :-

         18-pdrs.   60 rounds per gun.

         4.5" Hows.   45 rounds per gun.

         T.M's.   As many as possible

8. Attention is drawn to Air Photo No. 10.AC 279 of 27.10.17.

9. Zero hour will be at 1 p.m.

    All fire will cease at 3 p.m.

10. O.C. Left Group will render a full report on completion of this shoot.

11. Please acknowledge.

J.E. Marston

                                           Major R.A.
24.11.17.   Brigade Major, 38th Divisional Artillery.

Copies to :- 38th Division.   91st H.A.G.
             R.A. XV Corps.   115th Infantry Brigade.
             Centre Group.
             Right Group.

Army Form C. 2118.

WAR DIARY
INTELLIGENCE SUMMARY.
(Erase heading not required.)

121 Bde R.F.A.
for December 1917.

Place	Date	Hour	Summary of Events and Information	Remarks and references to Appendices
ARMENTIERES	Dec. 1917		During the first 3 weeks of December, Batteries and headquarters remained unchanged. Batteries in or near ARMENTIÈRES, headquarters at ERQUINGHEM, in charge of 2/Lieut Lynch. Our batteries shook our Sprenching occurred. The Front was very quiet. Details of two Prisoners shook are attached. Main W.D. Townsend R.F.A. commanded till 14th Dec. when Lieut. Col. Sparks relieved him. 8/30 Bde returning from camp. On the nights of 22/23 and 23/24 our batteries gave support in the "PRUDENT/WAIT" sector by battery of 7th Australian F.A. Brigade. The guns were taken over by the Aust. F.A. Brigade on the morning of 24th. The 115 Infantry Bde had previously been relieved by 3rd Aust. Divn.	AD 0078 AD 0080
			121 Batteries went into action as follows:	
			A/121 — Infantry battery at H.16 central —) under Left Group 30th DA	
			C/121 — forward — in H.23a	
			D/121 — (section in H.16.c	
			3 guns in H.24 b + d	
			B/121 Supporting battery in H.16c and 22a under Right Group.	
			121 Bde HQrs returned to SAILLY when Christian was Spares. and in 30th Dec. took over the HQrs 30th DA from 147th AFA Bde. HQrs at H.21.a 9.0. Batteries in the Group are A/121 — C/121 — D/121 — 97th Bk — 107 B-K — the Group cover the BOIS GRENIER section of the Divisional front held by 118th Infantry Bde. B/121, 107th Bk, and 3 guns of D/121 are towards batteries. 97th Bk — 11/121 and 1 section of D/121 in support at longer ranges.	
			During the month several stories have viewed the Brigade, including Capt A.H. Pocart who is 2nd/o in command to B/121. BSO Mr C was transferred to R.H.A. and now Commands Z battery. Major DC Stephenson	

1-17.D

Alex Clifton
Comd 121 Bde ??? Lt R.A

WAR DIARY
INTELLIGENCE SUMMARY
(Erase heading not required.)

Army Form C. 2118.

Y 21 Bde RFA Vol 25

Place	Date	Hour	Summary of Events and Information	Remarks and references to Appendices
In the Field	15th Jan		Brigade was still in action in the Fleurbaix sector under the Command of Lieut. Col. L.R. MacLellan DSO, R.F.A. & formed Left Group, 38th D.A. B/M. who attached to Right Group.	
	11/5th		Major J Ives of all Batteries moves from the Erquingham area further back towards Estaires. During the early part of the month nothing of any great importance took place. Retaliation to hostile Trench Mortars was carried very successfully. A fair amount of work was done towards strengthening Gun pits & Command Post men cemented.	
	17/18		The Divisional Artillery now relieves by 12th D.A. Gun pits & Wagon Lines being taken over accordingly. The Brigade then proceeds to back area to Haverskerque & Trains G.H.Q. Reserve. The two Batteries (A & B) proceed to Westrehem sector Ranges to calibrate then Gun.	
	21st		Remainder of Brigade's Batteries remained at Haverskerque & commence the usual training.	

Signed J.H. Bell Lt Col RA
Cmdg 121 Bde R.F.A.

Army Form C. 2118.

WAR DIARY
or
INTELLIGENCE SUMMARY.
(Erase heading not required.)

12 Bde RGA Feb. 1918.

Place	Date	Hour	Summary of Events and Information	Remarks and references to Appendices
HAVERSKERQUE.	Feb 1918		On Feb 1st the Brigade was still at rest: Brigade Headquarters and two Batteries at FONTAIN LES HERMANS + the two remaining batteries at HAVERSKERQUE. The two batteries at FONTAIN were calibrating on the WESTREHEM machine range where some successful shooting was carried out. On Feb 2nd the two batteries at HAVERSKERQUE marched to FONTAIN to relieve the two batteries which went there. On Feb 5th Brigade Headquarters + the two batteries marched back to HAVERSKERQUE. During the rest of the time there Brigade sports + competitions were held, into which the men entered with great enthusiasm. Drill + training were also carried out which greatly improved the efficiency + discipline of the troops. On the 16th/17th + 18th the Brigade marched to proceed into action were received. On the night of the 17th the relief of the 286th Bde in the Right Group was complete.	
ARMENTIERES.	18.2.18		The Group front now extends from 1.20d4.5.15 1.16b2.6, Sheet 36. Headquarters is at farm H17b 15.80., and batteries as follows — A/121 along road in H12c B/121 do do "H12b. C/121 along road in I7d. D/121 at +118a2.1.	

WAR DIARY
INTELLIGENCE SUMMARY

Army Form C. 2118.

121st Bde RFA
Feb 1918

Place	Date	Hour	Summary of Events and Information	Remarks and references to Appendices
	Feb-15.18		The hostile Artillery is Quiet. In war positions Silver Group (for example) are not shooting from same Positions as were in the shooting from some divisions from her positions. 196.— O.P.s are SPION KOP 17.d.6.2, and those in CHAPELLE D'ARMENTIERES with men which we had occasionally. (La PNE DU B.12.2 and MOSQUITO PALACE (LILLE POST) in I.15.6. No operation group positions have taken place on the group front since we took over: we have done a good deal of registering. Two T.M.s and 4" Mortars fire for a "prospective" raid. Wagon line taken over are those vacated by the 112th Punjab Artillery, near ERQUINGHEM, with Hrs on B.26.d.3.3. in January 1918, at L'EPINETTE, near ERQUINGHEM)	
	1-3-18			

[signature]
Lieut Col RFA
Cmdg - 121 RF Bde

Army Form C. 2118.

WAR DIARY
INTELLIGENCE SUMMARY

12 / Bde R.F.A.

March 1918

(Erase heading not required.)

Place	Date	Hour	Summary of Events and Information	Remarks and references to Appendices
ARMENTIERES	March 1918		The position of Brigade and Batteries are the same as for last month. The Brigade forms the Right Group of Bde Arty Artillery, and is defending the WEZ-MACQUART sector, South of ARMENTIERES, covering the 115th Infantry Bde.	
			Activities of the enemy and ourselves have been unremarkable during the month.	
			(i) Enemy activity. Between about 6th March and 21st March his sentries activity was quite abnormal. Compared chiefly to the smaller calibres. Enemy's heavy 77 battery and some field howitzers has been brought up to near 1st Camp at "Vingt"; for English mile men, the day of the firing of the Offensive with SOMME, activity died down suddenly. Beside sporadic shrapnel fire all day on forward areas, there was considerable harassing fire on back areas with batteries as well as my unmanned acting H.V. guns against villages and trains at back areas. ERQUINGHEM was constantly knocked about. His artillery activity was accompanied by unusual infantry liveliness. Storm troops were brought up on several occasions to carry out raids in the front of the Division. Only on such raid took place on our Brigade sector – that on the Early morning March 11th, when the Right of our line and the left of the Division in our Right, was raided. Unsuccessful frowns Many bombs were thrown but no our Brigade or our left.	
			9th/10th during a raid on the Brigade or our left.	
			The Enemy's activity culminated in the morning of March 28th, when about 5am O.Sos front of the Battery was carried out. On this Zone for about 3 hours. This first died at about the sector before it could would pass...	
			(ii) Our Own activity.	
			On March 2nd, at 11.50 pm, a raid of M.B. Kent and J.Inch Trench Mtr I.6	

2353. Wt. W2544/1454. 700,000. 5/15. L.D. & L. A.D.S.S./Forms/C. 2118.

WAR DIARY
INTELLIGENCE SUMMARY
(Erase heading not required.)

Army Form C. 2118.

127 Bde RFA

Place	Date	Hour	Summary of Events and Information	Remarks and references to Appendices
	March 24th		147 Bde. Hdqrs. (Central Group) was withdrawn on the evening March 24th. From 6 p.m. that day, Flying Group took over the front Eastwards as far as the Railway in I/1.a, covering the right of the 113th Inf.Bde. in H.5.b.5.5 & H.15a. & H.15d. 2 Bays for 113th Inf. Bde was withdrawn into reserve, and 115th Inf.Bde. took over the front Westward to the Railway with 3 battalions in the line holding H.1.2 as before. On 29th March the 115th Inf. Bde. were relieved in the VIZ. outpost line by a Bgd of 57th Divn, who were in turn relieved on the following day by a Bgd of 34th Divn, when our front became 30th Divn front & we have been withdrawn.	
	March 29th		From 16th March till 29th March, the Group on Bryan were commanded by Lieut.Col. Bish RoSS (Cmdg CJM.) during the absence of Lt.Col. S.P. MacClellan on a course in England. On March 27th, Capt. L. Harwood and Lieut R.A. Baker, C.O. of A/192, were evacuated to 61st D.H. and on March 29th, Lieut H.P. Hancock B/1/92, war Lieut H.T. Selby (B/192) returned on March 30th after been in hospital sick. He was wounded on July 31st at PICKEM. On March 1st Lieut E.J. Crowells R.F.A. joined the Bryad as Signal Officer, and Lieut T.D.T. Drouetchurst (to England sick)	

1-4-18

(Sgd) MacClellan Lieut Col RFA.
Cmdg 127 Bde RFA

WAR DIARY
or
INTELLIGENCE SUMMARY

Army Form C. 2118.

121 Bde. HQrs

Place	Date	Hour	Summary of Events and Information	Remarks and references to Appendices
	March 2nd		Programme for Artillery support to be attached with Super Carnival to ourselves.	(App. I.)
	March 10th – 15th		(b) On 10th March prisoners. Enemy's Officers were taken, with Enemy prisoners were taken, with super careful. Enemy's activity gave rise to the belief that an attack in the first night be imminent. Counter-preparation and Scheme of barrages commenced later were carried out from Stranghler of 10.57 PM (details of) 14/15th. H.A. Bombarded Enemy billets & rear communications. Scheme for attack.	Appendix II.
			(c) At 5.30 am March 9th. The Gunners believed (4 Men & 8 Guns C/122) assisted the 21st Div on our Right in a successful minor operation. Details are attached.	Appendix III.
	March 15th		(d) At 10.7 pm on March 15th the Bosch on our Left carried out a successful raid on INCHINDESCENT TRENCH and SUPPORT assisted by a barrage of the Rifle Group. Artillery programme is attached. Many prisoners were taken.	Appendix IV.
	March 18th		(e) At 11.10 pm March 18th A/122 assisted 12th Div. in a small raid in I.32.a. See attached notes.	Appendix V.
	March 28th		(f) On 28th March. 10th STAFFS. Raided the Enemy's line in I.21.c under cover of Artillery barrage with three by Rifle Group. Artillery programme attached. Casualties were knowingly carried out by all Batteries in 3 places. HQ that assisted in the raid. 6 prisoners were taken, our casualties were few.	Appendix VI.
	March 29th		(g) At 3.30 am. March 29th a Hostile raid on WEZ MACQUART. Was carried out on outposts Identification was 116th Regiment IOth Res Div. Was carried out by a storm troop of 10 who of the Guard, (and the front held by the 11th without difficulty under cover of a Gas Barrage. (Programme attached) but found it deserted.	Appendix VII.

38th Div.
V.Corps.

WAR DIARY

Headquarters,

121st BRIGADE, R.F.A.

A P R I L

1 9 1 8

INTELLIGENCE SUMMARY

121st Bde R.A.
April 1918

(Erase heading not required.)

Place	Date	Hour	Summary of Events and Information	Remarks and references to Appendices
ERQUINGHEM	9th		Brigade still in action as Right Group, 30th Div Arty, supporting & Brigade of 34th Div in the line — WEZ - MACQUART Sector.	
"		4.15 am	Heavy hostile bombardment with H.E. and Gas Shell opened on Brigade H.Q. and Battery positions. This was part of a General bombardment. Gas continued with lulls till about 10 pm.	
		10.30 am	Infantry Group retiring on our right. "A" Stats Group were within 800 yds. Battalion shortly to withdraw N of the LYS. At this time its Brig. R.A. & D Batteries intended to retire the Batty under heavy M.G. fire at short range West of Headquarters & early frontline via Railway through the position of D Battery and about 200x Rolanderie. 2 Howitzers of D Battery (at La Vesee) and one abandoned (This had been taken out of position by 34th D.A.) which was in progress of relieving 30th D.A. This unit was cancelled at 4pm.	
		1.15 pm	Headquarter was transferred to B Battery's position at the RUE MAPLE alternative position. By 4pm all batteries except the Brigade Group. Band C Batteries retired to position N of the LYS. Information received that enemy had crossed the LYS at BAC. S. MAUR and CROIX DU BAC. Fire on the river crossing that were around the road between their lines and by 6.10am next day	
		5 pm	during the night the new enemy retirement was	
		7.30 pm	A and B batteries moved to position between NIEPPE. Batteries were firing on the BAC S. MAUR Crossing and also at times	
	10th		on Infantry were firing near FLEURBAIX. Officer casualties — Killed — Br.Major W. Allinson (H.A.); Wounded Capt G.C. Lalanne Bance (H.A.) — Lt Fargue (D/121)	
		10.30 am	Brigade ordered to occupy position E. of STEENWERCKE. Rearguard was carried out by batteries last. Infantry was in position by 2pm. HQ. was STEENWERCKE Station.	
		2.30 pm	Batteries opened M.G. fire from both flanks and infantry retiring through them.	
		3 pm	M.G.'s were at close range, this being the infantry line. Batteries withdrew to position 500x NNE of Railway Embankment at STEENWERCKE Station, which was occupied by some infantry.	
		4 pm	2nd Worcesters and some Lewis Gunners of Northumberland and Lancashire Fusiliers. Fire was directed on STEENWERCKE - TROIS ARBRES road and along it and between it and the railway.	
		5.30 pm	2nd Hants Bn. arrived on BAILLEUL - NIEPPE Road	
		5.45 pm	Infantry on the railway line was E. of the Station. 2nd Hants reinforcing occupied line 200x N of railway, being reinforced by M.G.s and rifle fire from railway at range of 500x. Battalion HQ. was WITTELRAM in vicinity of BAILLEUL - NIEPPE road, where OC Brigade with BG. and 4, 88th Infantry Bde. on 29th Div.	

INTELLIGENCE SUMMARY

17th Bde H.Q. April 1918

(Erase heading not required.)

Place	Date	Hour	Summary of Events and Information	Remarks and references to Appendices
LA CRÊCHE	11th April	1.30 pm	Brigade around BRIGHTLOO who were defending line above STEENWERCKE Station. "B" and "D" Coys (platoons) relieved 1st Coys 35th Div. holding line S. of NEUVE EGLISE	
		2.30 pm	Brigade withdrew – 2 battalions at a time – to position E. of BAILLEUL more complete.	
BAILLEUL		6 pm	Bn. Headquarters now Grandgune.	
	12th		Brigade was covering 102nd & 147th Infantry Brigade, having a line through STEENWERCKE Station and PONT DE PIERRE to South of BAILLEUL Station.	
	13th	4 pm	Enemy attack drove in the L/F of 74th line. Infantry line was withdrawn to the line BAILLEUL Station, MONT DE LILLE, RAVELSBERG. Brigade withdrew by	
JAN S. CAPPEL	14th	10 pm	Larmore & position E. of ST JANS CAPPEL. 24th Div covering.	
	15th		Last farm by S. L.30 am. (176th Inf. Bde.)	
			(Green) 5th Div. MONT DE LILLE and RAVELSBERG.	
BERTHEN		6 pm	Enemy captured position by 7 am and was withdrawn to position 5 ft. on the evening of 15th, and rear to position N.	
		9.30 pm	34th Div. relief had relieved 5 ft.	
			1/BAILLEUL situation unchanged.	
	16th, 17th, 18th, 19th, 20th		Hostile attack were repulsed. Lt. J.C. Poole (B/17) wounded on 19th.	
	21st		34th British Div relieved by 133rd French Div.	
			Nature of position to be retained into a Brit Group of 4 Brigades (36th and 2nd N. Division)	
			Div. Artillery, Lewis CPBA, 3 pm H.Q. under the French. H.G. Hawkins (B/17) and Lt. R.F. Toilnt (B/17) wounded	
		10 am	23rd April. Div. Artillery & Brig. Exp. in front.	
			36th B.A. was withdrawn and 121st British Group 38th French.	
ABEELE	24th	8 pm	Very heavy enemy bombardment commenced on whole front.	
		11 pm	Brigade withdrew by lorries into bivouacs near ABEELE.	
HAMHOEK	25th	12 noon	Brigade marched to CRUBE at HAMHOEK.	
		1 pm	Orders received to march to position in readiness N. of RENIN & HELST.	

INTELLIGENCE SUMMARY

Dr B Mar April 1916

(Erase heading not required.)

Place	Date	Hour	Summary of Events and Information	Remarks and references to Appendices
RENINGHELST	25th	6.30 pm	Orders received to move into and occupy positions to the rear & S.W. of KASTEEL hill S. of RENINGHELST, about 1500 yds from the front line to support 25th Div in a counter attack in conjunction with the French on the Right and the 6th Div on the left, designed to re-take KEMMEL mount and village. Batteries were reinforced at dusk, and were occupied, and have now had our orders. Order for supporting Brigade. 1.15am — Divs have only 3 am and 74th A.Bde, 25th Bde (formed up to Bde H.Q at S.) attendance with A Bus. Batteries were constantly under shell fire and at 4 pm brigade was withdrawn by order to position N. of the GROOTEBEEK, covering 25th Div. Situation practically unchanged.	
	26th			
	27th 28th 29th	3 am	Heavy hostile bombardment commenced on whole Corps front. Enemy attacked always. Severe attacks on 25th Div. were repelled with our artillery fire. Batteries in action continuously from 3am till 9 pm. Firing about 2900 rounds per battery. Casualties during the day amounted to 7 killed and 12 wounded.	
	30th	1.30am 8pm	Brigade suffered a counter-attack by 25th Div in conjunction with the French on our Right to establish a line through the AUDOMPIER ESTAMINET (N14) on Left. Occasion 25th Div reached their objective but had to retire because the French failed to advance. Note D/121 Sustained heavy casualties during their withdrawal on 9th, and A Bty in action in the retirement near STEENWERRE station on 10th, in men or horses. Owing to road to that being blocked and to casualties in the teams, a certain amount of ammunition wagons had both abandoned — about 14 in all.	

MacCallan
Lt Col RA
O/c Frst/Art RA

Army Form C. 2118.

WAR DIARY
or
INTELLIGENCE SUMMARY.
(Erase heading not required.)

121st Bde R.F.A. Vol 7a May 1918

Place	Date	Hour	Summary of Events and Information	Remarks and references to Appendices
RENINGHELST	May 1st 1918		May 1st Turned the 121st Bde RFA (under 38th DA) still covering the front of 25th Divn in the neighbourhood of LA CLYTTE. On May 2nd the French began to take over the line, the relief of	
	4th		25th Divn by 32nd French Divn being completed on the night of 3/4 May. The 121st Bde RFA were came out of the Pont-Fixe - Huckenbush tramway and into rest.	
			The Field Artillery of 32nd J. French Divn took the Superpose upon that of the French Cattalie. Comersating about performance of fire to that we would not, but no major action.	
	6/7th		Arriving here on the 6/7 May the 121st Bde RFA. was withdrawn took up position was	
DICKEBUSCH	8th		BUSSEBOOM and come under orders of 33rd Divl Artillery. Group was artillery again on the night of 7/8 and Bg in position was DICKEBUSCH. On the morning of 8th May the Germans attacked	
			between RIDGEWOOD and the (SHERPENBURG). Our action "Peace prilling was then woken (Sunday 8th) and 103 Bde RFA (being in position) being ground broken local advance that this detach	
			sent for Captured Guns. Maj Wilson G/R Adamt on the morning of 8th this detach Headquarters and the Command staff up Hours - 600 to 9 am, 12 to 4 pm. Officers on duty	
			on the Bde - Hdqrs Adjt Seth: B/121, B-H Meyer, D/121, and the other being Capt ASKWITH C/121 and	
	9th		rest. B-H Meyer D/121, the other being relieved.	
	10th		On May 10th French troops began to come into the area in 11th the hoe paper in front of 5th & 7th 33rd Div were relieved by the 44 Br 14th French Bde, and on 12th the 121st Rdt	
			& other came under the of the French under Col. Lips commanding the Pile de 14th Divn.	
	11th		No incidents of great importance occurred. Except a combined attack by the French on Hill 44 Circle between the Scherpenb of the R-R. In attack the 121st Bde RFA fired very little, were previous	
			that was made before the advance, and retained being the Bed and moved on 9 Rainy day	
			Covering - Preparations Barrage was carried out daily, the S.O.C. barrage	
AARNOEKOT	13th		On the nights 14/15 and 15/16 the Brigade was withdrawn from the line to HAANDEKOT nr ADEN, and after a day or two of refit going at HAINEBEKE, on 18th the Brigade, strength of Battery & Rest billets at GERMINCOURT in DOWNERS.	

Army Form C. 2118.

WAR DIARY
~~INTELLIGENCE SUMMARY~~
(Erase heading not required.)

Place	Date	Hour	Summary of Events and Information	Remarks and references to Appendices
GEZAINCOURT	July		The time spent here was mostly given over to fitting out a little training. A parade of the entire Division was held on Sunday the 28th, and much individual work during the battle of the LYS was previously to obtain there.	
			The following decoration's have been awarded for operations during the last month:	
			Major H.L Hyett MC to Barto Military Cross.	
			Lieut. E.J Castello - Military Cross	
			Lieut. W.A.F. Grayston - Military Cross	
			Sergt. C. Bennett, D/D.M. - D.C.M.	
			and nine military medals.	

G.MacLellan
Lieut Col. RA
cmdg 70th Bde RFA

Army Form C. 2118

WAR DIARY
INTELLIGENCE SUMMARY
(Erase heading not required.)

121st Bde. RFA
June 1918.

JM 30

Place	Date	Hour	Summary of Events and Information	Remarks and references to Appendices
RAINCHEVAL	June 1st. Night 1st. 1/2/3		121 Bde RFA was in the RAINCHEVAL area preparatory to going into action. 121 Bde. RFA. relieved 62nd Bde. RFA (18th.DA.) in Silent positions covering ACHEUX sector (AUCHONVILLERS) and reinforcing 17th DA. BEAUSSART and MAILLY MAILLET. Wagon lines at PIDOC.O.2. behind ACHEUX Wagon lines were taken over from 17th DA.	121 Bde O.O. 21. 38 DA OO SS 17th. DA Den 193
	8th.		A certain amount of Calibration of guns was carried out. observing no fire until the Raid by 301th Inf. B.D. on night of June 8th. Copies parties and maps in attached. 30 Prisoners and 2 MGs were captured	Bde. O.Ost. 22. 17th DA O.O. No. 194
	9/10 10/11		A relief had been ordered between 121"R. RFA and 223rd BS RPA (63rd DA) who were to exchange positions — the latter was covering the Right of 38th DA. front in the MESNIL Sector. This however was Cancelled.	17th DA Oh. 196. 38th DA OO 60.
	10/11		On the night 10/11 the 121"R RFA was withdrawn from the 17th Dist from and batteries occupied vacated positions covering 38th DA. front — June 7 2 batteries going in the Right front and 2 in the left, then being 3 Brigades Vickers covering the Divil front. HQ. Of R.R. went with Brown.	
ENGLEBELMER	13th.		On 13th. June 121 Bde. Hdqs. took over the left Group 38 DA. covering 113 Inf. Bd. Orders were withdrawn and 121 Rd RFA exchanged positions with 232 (Army) Bde. RFA. Rhus left the 2 301th DA Brigade covering the 301th. Dist. front. Each with its own batteries. Positions his were as shown in 301th. DA. order No 60., with Group headquarters at P.24. d. 4. 4.	Or. Z.
	19/20.		In the night of 19th. 20th. June, a feint was made in the Ambry Wood sector in which 121 Bd. RFA. Co-operated, as shown in Left Group Order No Z 2 and attached hereto.	38 DA O.O. 64.

Army Form C. 2118

WAR DIARY
INTELLIGENCE SUMMARY

121 Bde, R.F.A.
June 1918

(Erase heading not required.)

Place	Date	Hour	Summary of Events and Information	Remarks and references to Appendices
ENGLEBELMER	June 21st.		At 2.5 am. 21st June a Raid was carried out by 2nd R.W.F. and 14th R.W.F. on the front between HAMEL and AVELUY WOOD. Telegraph Order 21 and 38 S.A.A. O.O. No. 63 on attached. Two prisoners from were captured and from 3 Mc.Guns Kills. During however, both parties had the trenches were practically deserted. No prisoners were taken.	Order 21, BRDA, O.O. 83
	22/23		On the night 22/23 June, 115th Inf. B.P. relieved the 113th B.P. in the Left Sub. and on 28/29 and 29/30 relieved it further to the Right. Divisional Boundary Western Divn. Front was held now by the Brigade, with our in Bethune and the this in Reserve. Harassing fire has been carried out by all batteries continuously, and casualties inflicted upon enemy working parties, especially in the Valley near BEAUCOURT which is in full view from the O.P. Several Sos shoots have been carried out on Valleys opposite line from D/101 Capturing Specimens on attacked. No fire carried out by T.M.'s under the Group.	Order 28 DJ, 85 19.0/28 14.6/23

R.A., 38th.Div.No.G.S. 1901/28

SECRET.
XXXXX

Left Group.)
Right Group.)
D.T.M.C.) For information.
S.C.R.A.,)

15th. June 1918.

Reference Sheet 57 D. 1/40,000.

1. On the night 16/17th. June a gas bombardment of VALLEY R.1.b. and d. and R.7.b. will be carried out, provided weather conditions are favourable.

The following artillery is taking part :-

    8. 4.5" Hows. covering 17th. Divl. front.
    2. 4.5" Hows. covering 38th. Divl. front.
  24. 6" Hows.

2. (a) O.C. Left Group will detail 2 Hows. for the task.
   (b) Concentration points (M.Ps.1.) will be as under :-

      (A) R.1.b.5.8.
      (B) R.1.b.5.5.
      (C) R.1.d.6.8.
      (D) R.7.b.5.9.

NOTE:- If the wind has a tendency to SOUTH, the M.Ps.1. should be engaged in order A to D, if a tendency to NORTH they should be engaged in the order D to A.

3. PROCEDURE.

TIME.	ACTION OF ALL GUNS.	NUMBER & NATURE OF SHELL
		B.N.C.
Zero to Zero plus 2 mins.	Target A or D.	4.
Zero plus 2' to Z plus 4'	Switch.	
Z plus 4' to Z plus 6'	Target B or C.	4.
Z plus 6' to Z plus 8'	Switch.	
Z plus 8' to Z plus 10'	Target C or B.	4. rds. per
Z plus 10' to Z plus 12'	Switch.	gun.
Z plus 12' to Z plus 14'	Target D or A.	4.
Z plus 16 to Z plus 2 hrs. 30 mins.	Distribute. (each target receives one quarter)	70.
Z plus 2 hrs.40' to Z plus 2 hrs. 50'.	Distribute.	16.

4. ACTION OF 60 pdrs.

60 pdrs. have been ordered to fire shrapnel on the area of the shoot from :-

Zero plus 2 hrs.40 mins. to Zero plus 2 hrs.50 mins.

5. A five minutes concentration of all howitzers that can bear, firing H.E. will take place at 4 a.m. and 8.50 a.m. on 17th. June.
(2 rds.p.g.p.m.)

6. Information as to whether weather is favourable or not and synchronised time will be sent from this Office at about 7.30 p.m.

7. Zero hour will be 10 p.m. the 16th. June.

8. Left Group ACKNOWLEDGE.

Major R.A.
Bde. Major 38th. Divl. Artillery.

WAR DIARY or INTELLIGENCE SUMMARY

Army Form C. 2118.

12th 8th Bde. R.F.A. July 1918

Place	Date	Hour	Summary of Events and Information	Remarks and references to Appendices
ENGLEBELMER	July 1918		The Brigade still in action as Centre B/A. left Group. V Corps. Believe 1st and 16th July. Lt-Col. G.P. Mac Clellan D.S.O. Commander 3 Bde. Div. A.K. whilst Lt Col GOC R.A. was on leave. Major M.D. Turner D.S.O. Commanded 12th A&B Bde R.F.A.	
	11/12		On the night 11/12 July, 2nd R.M.F. (115 Bde.) raid & successful raid on HAMEL whilst Capt.n 167 prisoners and a machine Gun 3 Bde D.A. Operation Bdes No. 67 is attached, and shows action of 12 Bde R.F.A.	O.O. 67
	12/13		On the night 12/13 July, 63rd Divn (on Left) carried out a raid in which the 15th R.F.A. co-operated. No 68 Bde of prisoners. See 3 Bde D.A. Order No 68 attached.	O.O. 68
			d'Iris was captured. See G.94 attached: an Germans discharged into HAMEL Action by in 17/18 July shortly from plan of enemy traffic routes opposite the Corps front. See R.A. 3D Bde No. G.S. 2146/30 attached.	G.94. GS2146/30
			The 3 Bde Division, on relieving was withdrawn into reserve on the night 18/19 July the two flank Divisions extending, their fronts to cover the Sector. 12 Bde R.M.F. and became Right Group, 63 W.DA. Supporting the 190th Inf Bde. Lt. 63 W. DA. OO. No 209 attached.	O.O. No 209.
	19/20		Details of the Rifles Group carried out by the 188 Inf. Bde. (Rfs on left) in which Group Cdn part, an attached.— Left Group 3D DA. Order No. 9.	Order 9.

Army Form C. 2118.

WAR DIARY
or
INTELLIGENCE SUMMARY.

(Erase heading not required.)

B.H.Q. R.H.A.   July 1918.

Instructions regarding War Diaries and Intelligence Summaries are contained in F. S. Regs., Part II. and the Staff Manual respectively. Title pages will be prepared in manuscript.

Place	Date	Hour	Summary of Events and Information	Remarks and references to Appendices
ENGLEBELMER	23/24		On the 23/24 July the 190 Inf.Bde. (63rd Div.) was relieved by 110 Inf.Bde. (21st Div.) came under the orders of C.R.A. 21st Division on my own 24/25 July. On 25rd, the 150 Inf.Bde. had advanced from his lines to the HAMEL - AUSLUY road and to the outskirts of HAMEL village. The 110 Inf.Bde. withdrew the two guns, owing to lack of invisibility	
	26/7 27/7		On the night 26/27, 27/28 July the 2 B.R.F.A's were relieved in the line by 94th B.R.F.A. (21st D.A.) and withdrawn into Rerun billets Harponville and Warloy.	2.F.D.A 0070
			Lieut. B.V. Clarke, A/171, was killed on July 24th, at the O.P. in BARN TRENCH, near MESNIL.	
	1-8-18			

[signature] Lieut Col R.A
Cmd. 121st B.B. R.F.A.

Army Form C. 2118.

WAR DIARY

INTELLIGENCE SUMMARY.

121 Bde. RFA

August 1918

(Erase heading not required.)

Place	Date	Hour	Summary of Events and Information	Remarks and references to Appendices
HARPONVILLE	August 1916 1st – 5th.		In billets at HARPONVILLE. Divisional Sports were held in the 3rd. and Divisional Race Meeting & Horse Show on 4th. In the latter, D/121 won the Driving Competition with 2 teams from our Battery.	
	5/6-8/7.		On the 5th. night the Brigade went into action relieving 78th Bde. RFA, 7th Div., in the AVELUY sector. Batteries took over positions near SENLIS (nur 2 Subsections) moved up towards BOUZINCOURT over to the Enemy withdrawal over the ANCRE a few days previously. Mount Kemil warfare prevailed during the first half of the month. The work which began on August 8th did no injury in wartime & A/121 BFA Major W? Wathen DSO M.C. (B/121) took command of the group (Brigade?) & was killed in mounting a lane.	
	18th.		On 18th August batteries were ordered to move up into the valley between MARTINSART and AVELUY Wood & support the attack by 21st Brig. on the Left up the ANCRE Valley towards MESNIL MONT and then Battery W. ANCROS opposite BEAUCOURT. This attack took place on 22nd & down.	
	23rd		Attack on 23rd August. 118 R?H. attacked up the Slope E ? AVELUY and Explosives and made good the hill. RUBBER LANE, and CROUCIX CORNER but was in Consolidation & on attack by 18th Div. on TARA HILL. The attack was supported by the Brigade.	
	24th.	1am.	At 1 am on 24th August a combined attack was carried out by the Divisions on the THIEPVAL – OVILLERS. LA BOISELLE – LA BOISSELLE Ridge. 18th Inf. Bde. attacked from USNA Hill in this direction of POZIERES, 114 Inf. Bde. in the same Division, about AUTHUILLE Wood. Their was Direct & converging attacks leaving a triangle containing both moped up the 115 Inf. Bde. The operation was successful the Division taking between 1000 & 2000 prisoners and 3 field guns, trench mortars, machine guns. By the Evening of 24th. No troops had reached the line COURCELETTE – POZIERES – BANIFF WOOD and attained a batteries. Pursuit was thereupon ordered and batteries	

WAR DIARY
INTELLIGENCE SUMMARY — 12 B.R. RFA   August 1915

Place	Date	Hour	Summary of Events and Information	Remarks and references to Appendices
	24th 25th	6 am	Munitions across the ANCRE near AVELUY battery lines of the morning & evening barrage was fired in support of 113th Inf. Bde. attack on CONTALMAISON. That valley was empty without opposition. At 6am the White Brigade moved the ANCRE and marched to join W. of Lt. Bn. Sqdn. awaiting orders from G.O.C. 113th Inf Bde. 113th Inf Bde held up C. Cie Nacorph MAMETZ WOOD with infantry. Reconnaissance showed BOTTOM WOOD entirely unoccupied in front of DIVISION on right with (no reinforcement in 76) x 15. The Brigade supported a further battery the same evening. Batteries will thereafter.	
	26th	5:30 am	When bombardment at 5.30am of enemy barrage was fired in support W.1 CONTALMAISON. 113th Inf. Bde. with the division of LONGUEVAL which was not reached through BAZENTIN LE GRAND and LE PETIT was captured. Returning to the enemy counter attacked and prepared or back a little in the evening. In X.17c and 18a in Bazentin by 20th Division. Was hard pressed advance in action unopposed towards LONGUEVAL. Batteries moved up in front of Bazentin le Petit.	
	27th		BAZENTIN LE PETIT. An hour an attack was made by 113th Inf. Bde. supported by the 7th on GINCHY but the opened beyond Little opposition was encountered and GINCHY was lightly held.	
	28th		An hour moved to the W of Lily of MORVAL where they were held up. 1 on factors CATERPILLAR VALLEY. DELVILLE WOOD. An attack	
	30th 31st	6pm	6pm. Failed on 30th at Dawn the weaponry was at spent in counter on 30th and have being fired as further infantry actions.	

Casualties with the Brigade have been high during the month.

R W Mathieson, Major RFA
Cmd 121 Bde RFA

Army Form C. 2118.

WAR DIARY
INTELLIGENCE SUMMARY.

121/Bde R.F.A.
September 1918

(Erase heading not required.)

Instructions regarding War Diaries and Intelligence Summaries are contained in F.S. Regs., Part II. and the Staff Manual respectively. Title pages will be prepared in manuscript.

WO 95/33

Place	Date Sept 1918	Summary of Events and Information	Remarks and references to Appendices
MORVAL	1st	Batteries moved to MOUCHOIR COPSE to support attack on MESVIL-EN-ARROUAISE.	
MOUCHOIR COPSE	2nd	Attack on night 2/3 Sept: failed. Batteries withdrawn to MORVAL. H.Q. to GINCHY as hostile Counter attack was anticipated. Enemy retired E. of CANAL DU NORD during the night.	
MOUCHOIR COPSE	3rd	A/121 + B/121 moved to position of readiness at MOUCHOIR COPSE. C/121 + D/121 into action forward of SAILLY SAILLISEL.	
SAILLY SAILLISEL A.K.	4th	A/121 + D/121 moved into action forward of B/121 + C/121. Infantry arrived the CANAL + H.Q. moved to SAILLY SAILLISEL	
ROCQUIGNY	5th	Further retirement of the enemy to beyond FINS. H.Q. + Batteries moved to position between ROCQUIGNY and BUS. relieving the Bde of the 21st D.A. and coming under 17th D.A.	
LECHELLE	6th	Moved to position of readiness near LECHELLE.	
YTRES.	7th	Crossed Canal du Nord to position S/LECHELLE	
FINS.	8th	Into action N. of FINS.	
	9th	Attack on AFRICAN TRENCH. AFRICAN SUPPORT gained.	
	10.	Came under 38th D.A.	
	15th	Moved up two batteries at a time S/o the road FINS - GOUZEAUCOURT. preparatory to	
	16th	Attack by 3rd, 4th + French Armies. 121 Supported 114th Infantry Brigade	
	17th		
	18.	+ gained the Tunnel Line S.W. of GOUZEAUCOURT.	

WAR DIARY
INTELLIGENCE SUMMARY
(Erase heading not required.)

Army Form C. 2118.

Instructions regarding War Diaries and Intelligence Summaries are contained in F. S. Regs., Part II. and the Staff Manual respectively. Title pages will be prepared in manuscript.

Place	Date	Hour	Summary of Events and Information	Remarks and references to Appendices
FINS.	September 26		Supporting 115th Infantry Brigade in the line W. of GOUZEAUCOURT.	
	21st		Came under C.R.A. 17th D.A.	
	22nd		Carried out Harassing fire on GOUZEAUCOURT area & Hindenburg Gun protection by K Special Coy R.E. with Gasshells.	
	23rd			
	24th		Came under 21st D.A. 2nd Division	
	25th 1 p.m.		Supported attack by battalions of 6th Bde 21st Div on AFRICAN TRENCH. attack successful.	
	26th			
	27.		Fired barrage in attack on GOUZEAUCOURT & positions which 1/21 Bde advanced about 2000 yards to positions N. of REVELON. Fired barrage in further attack by 21st Division coming under 33rd D.A. at Zero + 75 minutes. 5:30 a.m. fired barrage in support of attack on Green line & moved forward to position S. of VILLERS GUISLAIN. almost immediately to position E. of VILLERS GUISLAIN.	
	28.		Major W. M. Mathison D.S.O. 2nd in Command from attack to	
	29.		Major (M.D.) Townsend D.S.O.	
	30.		Lieut Col. G. F. MacClellan D.S.O. wounded from keen sniper fire slight during the month	

July 34
121 Bde. R.F.A.

Army Form C. 2118.

WAR DIARY
or
INTELLIGENCE SUMMARY.
(Erase heading not required.)

Instructions regarding War Diaries and Intelligence Summaries are contained in F. S. Regs., Part II. and the Staff Manual respectively. Title pages will be prepared in manuscript.

Place	Date	Hour	Summary of Events and Information	Remarks and references to Appendices
VILLERS-GUISLAIN	1st Oct.		Enemy retired to the River L'ESCAUT. Villages harassing fire carried out regardless of own.	
	2nd Oct		Section pushed forward to within 1500' of River.	
	3rd Oct			
	4th Oct			
LA TERRIERE	5th Oct		Came under 38th Div. Battery to provide LG's onto heights South of BASKET WOOD. R.H. Section carried on good work of firing at Coys. of C/121 in was to deepen back on S.H.G. & 2. Interim harassing fire and wire cutting during night.	
	6th Oct			
	7th Oct		Intense harassing fire and wire cutting carried out on the BEAUREVOIR LINE and	
MORTHO WOOD	8th Oct	6.30am	support. At 01.00 hours had 6 pdr 10 Barrage in support of attack on 113 Inf. Div on a two divisional front with 21 Div on the Left, 30 Aus Div on Right. The attack was successful and Batteries advanced to positions South of MORTHO WOOD. Fire which a lot of Barrage was fired at 11.30 hours.	
HURTEVERT FARMS N. of BERTRY	9th Oct	6 a.m.	Brigade moved to position R. Redman a T13 central a/05.00 hours. No word of enemy strength in T. & 4. 2nd movement from there to N.36 welfare Near Battery in O.21 near HURTEVENT FARMS and near those of P.T.E. road, North to Bridge.	
E. of TROISVILLE	10th Oct		BERTRY. Batteries moved to eastern K.31 near TROISVILLE to support the 98th Infantry advance movement.	
	11th Oct		River SELLE. Counter Battery work and Observed fire on movement.	
	12th Oct		150 H.V. & V. Battery 2 days with flashes End of RIVER, no enemy movement, attack dropped, high ground artillery.	

(10340) Wt. W5300/P713 750,000 3/18 B. 1688 Forms/C2118/16
D.D. & L., London, E.C.

WAR DIARY
or
INTELLIGENCE SUMMARY. 12 Bde R.F.A.

(Erase heading not required.)

Army Form C. 2118.

Place	Date & Hour	Hour	Summary of Events and Information	Remarks and references to Appendices
TROISVILLE	15th 16th	Oct.	On the night 15/16 Oct. Brigade was subjected to a violent Gas BOMBARDMENT, resulting in casualties of 12 O/Rs and 100 OR's. Battery positions approached and new ones in K.25.d.Q. being occupied.	
	19th	Oct.	Brigade moved to action in K.25 in liaison with 113 Inf Bde.	
MONTAY	21st	Oct.	Batteries crossed RIVER SELLE & action in K.16 N & MONTAY	
	22nd	Oct.	Supported attack by 33rd Bn. with Mormal FOREST as object.	
VILLERS	23rd	Oct.	Batteries moved to P.15 near SLAUGHTER HOUSE. Advanced to position Sq VENDEGIES-au-BOIS in Support of further attack entrusted by 38th Bn.	
PAUL JACQUES FARM	24th 25th	Oct.	Final Objective night new GAND. Batteries moved to action near PAUL JACQUES FARM.	
BERTRY	26th 27th 28th	Oct.	Brigade proceeded to rest at BERTRY at 11.30 hrs.	
	29th	Oct.	Brigade proceeded by train A/W C/W west of WARGNIES-LE- B/De SILT W F PONT-DU-NORD in relief of 223rd Bde. BHA.	
	30th 31st	Oct.	At N.W 30/31 Oct. a Gas Shell was experienced by this Bde 8 Jones Y/12 Wheeler Attached Ew.	

M.B.Lon R.A.
Lieut R.F.A.
Adjg 12th Bde R.F.A.
1.11.18.

Army Form C. 2118.

WAR DIARY
or
INTELLIGENCE SUMMARY

(Erase heading not required.)

121 Bde R.F.A. November 1918

W.D. 36

Place	Date	Hour	Summary of Events and Information	Remarks and references to Appendices
	Nov 1918			
POIX DU NORD	1st – 4th.		Batteries in action near POIX DU NORD, covering front ENGLEFONTAINE Southwards. Headquarters at VENDEGIES-AU-BOIS.	
	4th.	6.30a	Attack by 1st, 3rd, and 5th British and 1st French Armies commencing 6.30 a.m. 38th Div. attacked.	
HECQ.		7.15a.m	Supports to advance. About noon batteries advanced, and took up positions S. E. of HECQ	
		noon.	in the FORÊT DE MORMAL. Headquarters at HECQ.	
	5th.		Advanced through the Forest in support of 98th Inf Bde (33 Div), and took up positions S.	
SARBARAS			of SARBARAS for the night. Headquarters near CROISIL Inn. Our batteries and Headquarters going on to SARBARAS	
	6th.		Artillery came into action in support of SARBARAS, but could not cross the SAMBRE owing to the	
			destruction of all bridges. Advanced Guard infantry soon got out of range.	
	8th.		D/121, under 169 AFA Brigade, crossed SAMBRE at BERLAIMONT, and came into action	
			near ÉCUYE ECUELIN.	
	9th.		Brigade crossed SAMBRE at SASSEGNIES, and advance to HULK or DOURLERS, the enemy	
			having retreated and lost touch.	
	10th.	11h.	Moved to WATTIGNIES. Hostilities ceased 11 a.m. on Nov. 11th.	
	20th.		Moved to billets at AULNOYE Factory.	

[Signature]
Lieut Colonel
Comdg 121 Bde R.F.A.

30th

121 Bde R.F.A.
P/B 2607A
Dec 1918

O/I 36

WAR DIARY
or
INTELLIGENCE SUMMARY.
Army Form C. 2118.

Place	Date	Hour	Summary of Events and Information	Remarks and references to Appendices
AVELUY	Dec 1 to Dec 28th Jan 1st 1919		Quietness was spent at AVELUY Moved via NEUVILLE, FRANVILLERS, MIRAUMONT, ALBERT to PONT NOYELLES (nr Amiens). Arrived at hutted Camp on Jan 1st 1919 All good meals were served & every man got sum's to drink	

J. Hay Cullen
Lieut Col RA
Cmdg 121 Bde R.F.A.

Army Form C. 2118.

121 Bde R.F.A.

WAR DIARY
or
INTELLIGENCE SUMMARY
Jan 1919
(Erase heading not required.)

Place	Date	Hour	Summary of Events and Information	Remarks and references to Appendices
PONT NOYELLES.	Jan 1.		Arrived in hutted Camp PONT NOYELLES, where the Month was spent. Demobilisation Drew + lorries Commenced.	

A.T. Barker
Major RFA
Comd. 121 Bde RFA

Army Form C. 2118.

WAR DIARY
or
INTELLIGENCE SUMMARY

12. Bde. A.F.A.
Feb. 1919.

(Erase heading not required.)

Place	Date	Hour	Summary of Events and Information	Remarks and references to Appendices
PONT-NOYELLES	Feb. 1919.		The month was spent in batteries. Guns and ammunition wagons were parked at Brit. CADRE park at GLISY. Demobilization of Men & horses continued.	

A.H. Borden
Major R.A.
Cmdg. 12 Bde. A.F.A.

WAR DIARY
or
INTELLIGENCE SUMMARY.
(Erase heading not required.)

121st Brigade R.F.A. Army Form C. 2118.
38th (Welsh) Divisional Group of Cadres.

Place	Date	Summary of Events and Information	Remarks and references to Appendices
PONTNOYELLES	March 1919		
	1st–5th	Major A.H. Peskett. M.C. commanded the Brigade until 5th March.	
	6th March	Major P.M. Balfour M.C. assumed command on the transfer of Major A.H. Peskett. M.C. to home establishment.	
	12th March	13 N.C.O's & men sent to U.K. for Demobilisation.	
	15th March	92 N.C.O's & men sent to U.K. for Demobilisation.	
	16th March	Major P.M. Balfour M.C. transferred to Home Establishment.	
	17th March	Capt. L. Powell M.C. assumed command.	
	19th March	Major F.H. Duckham assumed command on return from leave in U.K.	
	20th March	Brigade reduced to CADRE 'A' Establishment. Capt. L. Powell M.C. proceeded to U.K. for Demobilisation.	
	31st March	Brigade moved from PONTNOYELLES to Hutments at GLISY.	
GLISY		During the month the Demobilisation of Brigade was proceeded with. Strength of the Brigade remained good.	

Frank Wark Capt. R.F.A.
Adjt. 121st Brigade R.F.A.

Army Form C. 2118.

WAR DIARY
or
INTELLIGENCE SUMMARY.
(Erase heading not required.)

WL 40

Place	Date	Hour	Summary of Events and Information	Remarks and references to Appendices
GLISY	1-4-19		Major T.H. Duckham was in Command of the Brigade. The first few days were spent in settling down to the new camp at Glisy & clearing up the vacated one at PONT-NOYELLES. Sports & Football Cadre Competitions were played off. The Brigade being down to Cadre 'A' very few first men were demobilized. The health of the Brigade was very good & no serious case of illness was reported.	

Graystone Capt.
Adjt 121st Bde R.F.A.

www.ingramcontent.com/pod-product-compliance
Lightning Source LLC
Chambersburg PA
CBHW080848230426
43662CB00013B/2047